A LITTLE *MORE* LIGHT FROM THE STARS

A LITTLE *MORE* LIGHT FROM THE STARS

Warren Sunkar

Copyright © 2020 Warren Sunkar

The moral right of the author has been asserted.

All rights reserved.

No part of this publication may be reproduced, stored in a retrieval system, or transmitted, in any form or by any means, without the prior permission in writing of the publisher, nor be otherwise circulated in any form of binding or cover other than that in which it is published and without a similar condition including this condition being imposed on the subsequent purchaser.

 A catalogue record for this book is available from the National Library of Australia

Creator: Sunkar, Warren, author.

Title: A little more light from the stars / Warren Sunkar.

ISBN: 978-0-9953716-3-7 (paperback)

Layout: Pickawoowoo Publishing Group
(Interior and cover)

Contents

Creative Works 1

In The Light Of Sol 3

The Oracle 5

On A Starry Night 16

Thinking In A Thoughtless World 19

Love In A Living Moment 22

Wow 27

The Left-Hand Path 33

Running Back Up The Mountain 35

Strange Times 43

Esoteric Articles 47

Author's Note 49

An Awakening Planet 50

The Nature Of Contact 58

It's Time To Make Our Choice 66

Opening Our Ancient Eyes... 73

Cosmic Parasitism.. 84

The Alien Takeover Bid 95

How We Are Being Used To Enslave Ourselves........... 107

A Silent War..120

A Maddening World 137

The New Horizon..156

CREATIVE WORKS

IN THE LIGHT OF SOL

Standing upon a hillside, the faint glow of love christens the dawning horizon.

Silence, the womb of subtle expectation as nature holds its breath for this moment…

The first ray of light breaks upon the horizon releasing a wave of subtle love that washes all before it. A kookaburra breaks into laughter and in sweet symphony nature comes alive in chorus.

The sun's ray sweeps through my being in a gentle rush of bliss and I have become transparent in its light. I breathe deeply, the liquid plasm of Sol runs through my bodies, lighting and activating the Krystal temple of the brain. My heart has become a diamond absorbing and sharing the living rays of cosmic Light.

I attune my breath; harmonising with the Earth and Cosmos. Plasma accretes through me as I bathe in ecstatic bliss, igniting the divine chalice of fire as the warm elixir of delicious liquid light washes through my being.

Truly the new day is here…

The golden sun peaks over the horizon as more light sweeps the sky.

Would you believe that the living sun speaks to those raised to its consciousness? It shares its love with those who would partake in the uninhibited dance of Life. It whispers that the great change is here and my body pulsates in relief as its love softly penetrates my being, washing clear those obstructive energies in the liquid warmth of soft flowing ecstasy.

Nature is now singing her joy. Through my being I channel the subtle currents of New Life, they permeate the Earth and she receives them in love, clearing and bathing her in cosmic Love.

Now I turn inward…overflowing with divine joy into the heart of a sleeping humanity.

My whispers of love permeate their dreams… "Awaken children of light, the day is now here.

"Release from the night and leave the momentum of your subconscious dreaming. I am the voice of One calling you through the clouds of yesterday's fancy that keeps you slumbering in the lower substrate."

The light of Sol now breaks through their inner worlds and I rejoice, as the children of Love gently stir in their beds with smiles upon their faces.

The Great Mother kisses softly their cheeks.

They know the time is now…

THE ORACLE

It was midmorning as I trekked through a lush green Australian forest.

It was a magical day. Birds and insects were in beautiful orchestra. The dew still sparkled like small diamonds from the ends of the balgas and the morning sun gently warmed my face. The rich moist aroma of the forest permeated the air as I made my way through the giant karri and jarrah trees with no real thought of a destination.

I stopped for a moment to rest against a carpet of green tree moss that blanketed a fallen timber, when a small and nimble bird darted straight past my surprised face. Landing on a tree branch only metres from where I was standing, the little red breasted robin let out a flurry of sharp chirps to seemingly get my attention.

I watched it curiously as it took off into the air to somersault and land back on the branch before me. As I watched its display of cheerful aerobatics I felt a soft and gentle surge of uplifting energy wash through my body. Letting out another flurry of chirps the robin joyfully hopped and then darted off down a small leaf-covered track and I followed.

There was not a doubt in my mind that the bird was leading me somewhere as we made our way over logs and through the trees. The robin darted from branch to branch, upon which it would stop and chirp at me. Never getting too far ahead and often joyfully somersaulting through the air as it went.

To my surprise the trees started to thin out quickly into the green pasture of a large overgrown paddock. As I walked over the rotting post of a fallen and corroded wire fence line, I could see an old and derelict timber house. The red breasted robin was hopping around on a branch of a karri giving an exquisite series of chirps then it swiftly darted away towards the building.

As I made my way to the house I observed the remnants of an old overgrown garden. An assortment of flowers littered the area, wild, yet still flourishing around the collapsed and weathered building. It seemed to have been abandoned for decades.

The robin dashed past me once again to rest on the old rusted water tank next to the house and began to tweet very excitedly to me. Then with a final chirp it darted off around to the back of the house.

I was very curious...

As I followed around the side of the building, I noticed the garden became even more untamed yet more resplendent in colour as it merged with a small wood of trees behind the house. The atmosphere had become lighter and had an ethereal quality to it, almost dreamlike and beautiful.

I looked through the assortment of colourful flowers blooming around me which revealed a tall weeping willow tree at the back of the garden. To my surprise, hanging from one of its large branches was an old rope swing and on it sat a young girl with long black hair, dressed in a gown of white and wearing a purple hooded jumper.

I looked over her as she gently swung back and forth, her face hidden by the hooded jumper. She did not make a sound.

I guessed she would be in her latter teenage years.

I stood there a little perplexed, not knowing what to think of the situation and wondering why this young female was out here, by herself, in the middle of nowhere.

Then with a chirp and the feeling of wind against my cheek, the robin darted past me once again to land on a branch just above the young girl.

The girl's swinging came to a slow stop. Her face only very partially revealed as she looked up at the bird with a smile. It was tweeting very loudly and excitedly.

I started to walk up to her when her words stopped me in my tracks.

"I have been watching you Warren Sunkar."

She was looking directly ahead of herself and her face was again hidden.

I was immediately taken aback by the intent and power behind those words. I wondered how she knew my name. I was confused and just stood there wondering what to do or say next. I had no idea of who or what was talking to me.

"I have been watching you Warren Sunkar," she repeated. "You are not one of my own."

There was great power in her words but I did not feel at all threatened.

Her head turned slightly and her eyes peered through the partially opened hood as she looked at me curiously. "What are you doing here?" She asked. I felt her aura expand into mine and permeate the entire garden with a wash of her ancient but very uplifting presence.

I stayed silent, a little perplexed and in awe. Words would not come...

I knew this young girl was an oracle for whoever was really addressing me.

The atmosphere then lightened around us and I relaxed my being feeling a deep love stir in my heart. A strong wave of beautiful energy washed through me and then I knew exactly by whom I was being addressed. Before me, coming through this young girl, was the spirit of Mother Earth.

The girl then elegantly rose from the swing, her face still partially hidden under the hood that she wore. I could feel and see a soft ethereal glow emanating from the girl's being, gently washing the plants and trees around her. In the bliss of her presence I could hear the flowers singing.

She took a few steps further towards me. Her movement smooth and graceful as a colourful butterfly lifted from a nearby tree leaf and flew by her. I could see her smile at it with such deep love and affection that my own heart felt like it was blossoming. There was such tenderness in her gestures as she stood there marvelling like an innocent child as the butterfly danced and fluttered around her.

I felt her softly whisper to my deeper being as she enveloped me in her radiance.

We shared a silent exchange.

The energies were warm, safe and very joyful, touching my heart like a gentle kiss that raised my being to an exquisite feeling of sweetness and affection.

In response, I felt a surge of divine light come from above as an aspect of my greater being came down to anchor into my body. I spoke. "I have come from very far away to be here.

I have come to let you know that it is time."

She stood silently before me. I felt her momentarily take in deeply what was being said.

Suddenly I felt a slight tremor of sorrow wash through me. This time I felt a deep sadness in her voice. She asked softly, "What about my children?"

I stood there silent.

Again I felt a tremor of sorrow wash through me and her words became a little more demanding as she asked again, "What about my children?"

"It is time." I answered.

"No!" She spoke and this time I felt the tremor of a deeper pain go through my body and a rejection of my words. The atmosphere momentarily changed and went a little darker as a wave of energy washed through me that made me feel nauseous.

The young girl took another step towards me but then seemed to lurch forward in an unbalanced way. I stared at her, not really comprehending what was happening.

It was then I knew that something was not right. I could feel a deep pain within me as she stumbled. She seemed sick and as her aura darkened around her, I felt another strong wave of nausea. She staggered a step forward and she looked up at my face in deep pain. I looked into her eyes as her hood fell back around her shoulders.

What I saw next I didn't expect. My heart swelled heavily and a cry escaped from my mouth. I fell straight to my knees exhaling in my deep sadness.

She looked straight into my eyes; her face was no longer hidden. On one side of her head was a dark shadow that seemed to pulse through her body and I knew she was in great pain.

Tears openly ran down my cheeks as I saw the horrific truth and I could only watch her helplessly.

The girl's aura went dark and I felt like purging. I watched this dark unnatural frequency pulse around the side of her head; she cried out desperately in her confusion and distress.

My mind's eye played a vision of what certain alien realities were doing to her as toxic tar-like energies washed through her like poison. I saw alien machinery on both Earth and from beyond contorting and crippling her, sending pulses of artificial frequencies through her body. I witnessed the devastating effects of what an ignorant humanity have been doing through their negligence and greed. It was killing her.

Helplessly on my knees I watched her writhe and my heart ached for her.

And then I heard the plea of a desperate mother... "What about my children?"

I watched her with both great admiration and sadness. Even now, with all that her humanity was doing to her, she loved them so tenderly and so deeply. She would not give up her children and I knew, if necessary, she would die for them.

I felt overwhelmed and despairing. I knew that this so-called modern civilisation mostly didn't care.

I searched my being for the words I needed. To say something that would comfort her and relieve her great pain. I did not want to fail her.

I pleaded, "I have come to remind you of your family amongst the stars and the love that awaits you there. It is time, the greater shift must come."

She rejected what I was saying. "I will not leave my children."

I held her gaze. I could sense what she was doing; she was giving her children time. I knew she was far from powerless – with one shake she could clear much of her surface and much of her pain would be gone.

Another dark pulse rippled over the side of her face and her aura went dark and again she lurched and convulsed in agony as she wailed.

For a while I stayed silent, I did not know what to do. I could see she had been stripped of so much. I cried again, I felt like a helpless idiot. This was all so surreal and dramatic but I knew the reality of what I was seeing.

No words could be written or uttered for what I was feeling. My bones ached with sadness.

In desperation words broke from my lips. "Mother can you not feel that I love you. There are many of us who have come from so far away for this time to sing with you. We are here because we promised to come back for you because it is time you re-join us."

With effort she regained her composure and was listening to me.

I continued, "Feel this heart, you cannot stay here.

Those of your earth children who wish to come can come if they truly want to. We who have come from the stars love and remember you. I am here to remind you of your place with us. We the children of Love are waiting for you."

She smiled softly at me and there was such sadness. I could see the remembrance and hope glinting in her eyes. In her torture, in her grief, she had almost forgotten who she really was.

As she opened to what I was saying, she seemed confused and then looked down at her body self-consciously. She then looked up at me and wept in deep shame. I could see with my inner vision her horror of the damage done to her. Our Mother Earth who was once known as the blue jewel of our solar system had been stripped and desecrated. It was nothing short of rape.

I cried again and looked into her deep ancient eyes.

But there, behind her pain, I could see her even greater determination.

In that moment, I was moved by her beauty. I would do everything I could to help her.

I whispered to her as she cried, with tears streaming down my face, "You have nothing to be ashamed of beautiful mother...especially you."

We held our gaze on each other.

I looked upon her with nothing but the deepest love and strongest admiration.

She regained her composure.

Then she walked over to where I was kneeling and standing over me placed her hand lovingly on my cheek.

I looked up and sensed things I cannot explain. That she would endure all that she could and beyond for those she so loved. She had chosen her path and staring into her eyes I felt deeper possibilities that were hidden far from my sight. In those deep ancient eyes I felt my smallness and my blindness.

Words stumbled from my lips and I asked her as would a little child, "Open my eyes, my dear mother."

As she stood over me, I saw such a fierce resolution.

But I just wanted her pain to end.

"Soon," I whispered to her, "this will all be over and this passing age will be nothing but a fading memory. Things will be restored."

And I smiled at her and thought, and what is an age but perhaps a day, to one such as you.

She smiled back at me again as her hand gently trailed down my cheek. After a long moment of silence, she then turned to face the woods behind her and I watched her disappear like a fading dream into the trees.

I remember a deep tiredness washed through my body and I softly dropped, falling asleep in the warm, damp soil of the garden around me…

***

Hours later, I was gently aroused from my slumber by the young girl. She had no memory of the morning's events and explained to me that sometimes she would come to this place to be alone. As we talked and shared our experiences of the day, I knew we would become good friends.

As the afternoon sun slowly made its way downwards, we sat staring out over the paddock.

The oracle took my arm and rested her head on my shoulder as the small red-breasted robin sung sweetly from a nearby tree.

I shut my eyes but found little solace.

I laid down a hand on the soft earth beneath me.

And I thought:

It has been hard watching you humanity, polluting and tearing up the planet with no conscience or shame. Is it so hard to take the time out from your foolish little lives, to walk into nature and rest your hands upon your beautiful Earth?

Then tears began to swell as I remembered.

Just let her know that you care…

ON A STARRY NIGHT

I sat on a chair looking out over the paddocks where I lived. The sun was setting and I pondered over the many strange and unexpected events that had happened to me in recent years.

My life had been turned upside-down, having walked through an exploding public minefield of insinuations, blind accusations and deception from those who should have known better. People trying to make names for themselves with no care about the damage they were doing and totally oblivious to the deeper events that were happening around them.

I sighed.

Those who are unwilling to face their inner pain will often attack those who don't affirm their personal constructs of reality. Over the years I had come to know the madness of the world very well.

I watched the sun disappear behind the darkening pastures.

A Little *More* Light From The Stars

It had felt good to walk away once again from the clambering and chaos of human egos. It had been time to leave those who could not hear the new call of Love that was being gently sounded beyond their personal horizons.

Darkness gently fell upon the land before me. I sat watching the spritely twinkle of the first stars that appeared in the night sky. As I stared out into space the firmament quickly burst forth with its bright adornment of sparkling diamonds. It was magic.

There, under the soft luminescence of the Milky Way, I wondered what the coming days would bring.

With this thought, I saw two stars detach from the night just above the darkened skyline. Shining magnificently, these two silent UFOs shot forward from the distance speeding directly towards me. I stood up out of my chair as they stopped very close, just above the veranda and I then watched them make a sudden shift of direction as they hurled themselves upwards into the sky.

I laughed as a beautiful energy gently surged through my being. Striving upward in an arc of beautiful streaming light they played and danced with each other in a double helix configuration.

My heart felt as if it was rising with them and I felt the worries and cares of this maddening world fall away from me.

Then in a bright flash, they disappeared.
I kept staring out into the vastness of space.
And I smiled.
In the presence of the Cosmos, how can one not be sweetly humbled by one's own insignificance…

THINKING IN A THOUGHTLESS WORLD

We sat on a bench on an urban corner. I watched in amazement as hundreds of people held up their digital cameras and mobile phones taking pictures of themselves in front of a small city monument.

My friend Jahve sat next to me browsing the day's newspaper. As he read he spoke in a concerned voice. "They are saying here that scientists are going to release thousands of satellites into space and blanket the entire Earth in Wi-Fi and other artificial signals. They are saying that an amazing new world of connection and unlimited possibility is opening to us.

"What do you think about that?" he asked.

I looked at him. "Hmmm...you ask me what I think?

People do not understand that a devil can pose as an angel of light or a murderer can often smile and say kind things, especially when grooming his prey. The superficial and unthinking will lead each other into the same pit, too careless to pay attention and blinded by the bright lights and neon flashing around them."

Pondering a little more on what the newspaper had stated, I then repeated, "You ask me what I think?

That hell is but a state of psychic distortion, of realities misaligned from Life and fallen into inversion. It seems that here in Lucifer's playground people live in such deep self-absorption that they are too enthralled with themselves to care about the prison that is being built around them. Here, hell is a virtual reality game that is fun to engage and with many worlds to explore or to conquer."

It was then a young woman walked over and stood just in front of us and to our surprise began removing most of her clothing. Pulling out an i-Phone on a long selfie stick she sat up on the monument and began to pose seductively, presumably, to all her online followers. Her face was covered in make-up, her cleavage pushed forward and in a very tiny bikini she pouted and blew kisses at her camera.

We looked at her amazed. She did not seem to care about all the people gathered around and some of the cruder males whistled and encouraged her. She was playing in all the attention!

I looked back at Jahve. "You ask me what I think?

That no one is really thinking and they have all 'outsourced their brains'. That everyone has become so inherently disconnected from Life that they and their realities are becoming ever more retarded. Though I'm certain if you would ask one of these fools the same question as they stare at their own images and reflections, I'm sure they will tell you that hell has never looked so good!"

He looked up at me from his newspaper and said, "Some of us are in big trouble aren't we?"

I just stared at him and said, "You think?"

LOVE IN A LIVING MOMENT

Dust particles danced in the light of the sunlit window. My friend smiled as I walked into the room.

That week there had been a steady precipitation of higher energies and currents which had brought a subtle change of direction to an awakening experience we had been unfolding into.

It was a soft call of the soul that had called us together.

Life energies gently surged through my being and her beautiful eyes sparkled with a receptive shine. There was no need to speak because everything was seen in the living moment.

We drew close as she looked into my eyes with such purity of being that my heart opened and rejoiced as I met her beautiful gaze.

Gently touching her face, subtle electric currents flickered between us in a soft transmission of love. Safe and relaxed in each other's presence, we had nothing to hide from one another.

My spirit was tenderly stirred as she opened her being to me as a soft song of love played upon the ethers. Playfully we smiled to each other as we began to undress.

With a glance she beckoned me to the other room and I followed. I picked up a small candle and matches from the sunlit window sill as we went.

We then sat cross-legged on the floor, naked and unabashed before each other.

A light and beautiful energy washed through the room as we looked into each other's eyes. I lit the small candle and placed it next to us as we shut our eyes to give thanks to the Divine Mother. Her gentle and pervasive presence blessed the space. With soft ethereal whispers of light, we could feel protective gentle spirits dance into the room.

The ritual was sweet and touching yet it was our openness to life that evoked the living spirit to play with us.

As we came back to meet each other's gaze, I gently brought her on top of me as she wrapped her legs around my body. I did not enter inside her. There were no expectations or attachments, just the beating of our hearts and the offering of ourselves to God.

Together we embraced with a delicate kiss.

Slowly, rhythmically we harmonised our breathing, inhaling and exhaling as we let go of our surroundings. Unfolding yet simultaneously merging, we gently collapsed into a still point that lifted us both into resonance with the cosmic breath.

Our breathing gradually went deeper as we gently clasped each other's bodies though almost not conscious of doing so. Together, we slowly looked up in unison, releasing into a realm beyond time and space, losing the relativity of our body consciousness.

Allowing the breathing to rise in a crescendo, lifting our energies higher through our bodies, we let them collapse in unison. As one our energy fields opened in delight, unfolding as a cosmic flower.

Beautiful living light gently radiated from above. We raised our hearts to meet this sensuous space as the energy flowed down, fluid and delightful.

Our bodies began to pulsate, her legs wrapped tighter around my torso and she rubbed firmly against my body. Our subtle bodies pulsed as one, the energies of life swirled around us in a vortex of colour and I felt a glow of energy lift from my base washing upward through us to meet the downward flowing energies pouring through our crown in a splashing of soothing ecstasy.

My mind's eye opened as we were transported into a cosmic rapture. We started to dissolve in a suspension of time as we were lifted high into the exquisite love of the Cosmic Mother. Flowing, glowing and spinning in a thrilling dance of unspeakable bliss. Divine spirits of Life crowned us in a euphoric dream as light pulsed through us in a joyous wave.

I felt the throbbing of my physical body somewhere far below. Then in a pleasing orgasmic surge of energy which released through my heart, I felt the powerful rush of liquid light through me…

It released.

In a timeless peak we dissipated into nothing and everything.

As we drifted down back into our bodies, we exhaled deeply as we softly collapsed into each other physically. Sweat glistened over our skin in the soft candle light. Then slowly as we met each other's eyes in such joyous acknowledgement, we expelled our breath which released us into a deep relaxation as we gently fell backwards to lay on the floor. Her legs still wrapped around me as her naked arched body found the soft rug.

Then, deeply inhaling and exhaling we let go and released the experience as we lay there in silence.

There a long, sweet and euphoric moment passed, we were regenerated and thrilled. Smiling in elation and wonder as the divine energies very slowly and tenderly dissipated…

***

Hours later, I sat bare-chested on the balcony taking in the sweet smelling rose that was in my hand. My friend was still naked and looking out over the world. The warm rays of the sun illuminated her body.

She spoke as she pondered, "It makes you wonder what people are doing, they have forgotten so much!" She looked at me with a loving smile watching me smell the rose.

"The true tantra is the dance with Life. It is you communing with that rose, it is me dancing with the rays of father sun, it is us opening to God. What people are forgetting is that every moment is a living moment…" she spun around in a pirouette to face me.

I looked at her fondly. She was radiant.

"In this world people think it is another that gives them happiness and so they take it from each other. They have forgotten the blessing of pure Life that would dance in their hearts if only they would stop clinging so hard to that which is confusing them. True sex has always been a divine communion."

She replied, "It's so crazy isn't it, all this debased love only leads to pain and so much misunderstanding. How did our world get so twisted? I feel like shouting to everyone, just wake up…what are you doing?"

I laughed. "They would look at us as if we were the idiots. Perhaps they are not ready?"

She looked at me with a beautiful smile.

"Well, they are the idiots because they don't know what they are missing!"

She jumped into my arms and we broke into laughter.

WOW

My friend Kate came to visit the newly built apartments where I was briefly residing in a South-East Asian country. It was very hot and humid so we hurriedly removed her bags from the taxi and after saying goodbye to the driver, I took her into the air-conditioned complex where I was staying.

Taking out my security pass I slid it over a small sensor which opened the gate and we passed by the security guards in their windowed room who were monitoring the complex through their CCTV cameras and screens. They smiled and saluted as we walked past.

She looked at them a little reserved. We both come from the countryside of Australia and were not used to such formal protocols and security measures. We quickly walked into the apartment lobby where there were plush leather seats and couches that adorned the space with lighted fountains that glowed artificially opalescent. There were many large pot plants throughout the area and lining the walls.

She looked around and then looked at me. "Wow," was all she said.

Then walking towards one of the tropical pot plants she reached out and touched it but only to recoil. "It's fake," she said as she looked at me questioningly.

I laughed at her surprise. "They are all fake." I gestured at the entire room and she looked around the lobby frowning, reassessing what she first thought to be real plants.

"These modern apartment complexes boast cleaner and more sanitised living in Asia than what has been available over the last decades," I said. "These are the so-called new eco housing developments that are springing up all around here and the rest of the country." She looked at me in disbelief.

"Come, let's get up to the apartment." I smiled.

We walked out of the lobby, passing many posters on the wall that showed people in recreation. 'This Is Living' was written in bold print on them, referring to the apartment complex we were in.

I took out my security key and swiped the glass security doors as we continued to walk to the elevators.

As we stepped into the elevators, I swiped my security key again over a small pad before typing the floor number we were in. As we ascended to our destined floor the elevator wished us a good day. We then walked down another hallway lined with barred metal doors to reach our apartment. Placing my finger on a biometric pad on the door it read my fingerprint, then it opened and we walked inside.

The apartment was very small but tidy. I had been renting it the last couple of weeks from a website that I had found on the internet. In the centre of the main room was a large TV which, according to a small booklet beneath it delivered Wi-Fi, karaoke and other sorts of conveniences and amusements. Besides that, the rooms were sparsely furnished, air-conditioned and fitted with various smart appliances and lighting.

I smiled at her, "Why don't you have a shower and get changed," as I pointed to her room. "And when you are done join me out on the balcony."

She smiled back glad at the offer, needing to refresh after her flight.

About half an hour later she walked out of her room refreshed. I was sitting on a chair on the small balcony lined with artificial grass and flowers as she came through the curtained glass doors to join me.

She looked out from the balcony. "Wow," was all she said.

We looked out over a large pool that resided in the centre of the apartment complex. Palm trees lined the pool and as the sun was going down there were many small fountains lit up around the complex that started to change colours. In the distance, we could hear the crashing of waves and between the buildings see the ocean in the distance.

She looked at me with a frown and said, "I didn't know we were that close to the ocean?"

"We aren't," I replied. She looked at me a little weirded out.

"What you see is part of a projected illusion of water from a screen between those two buildings," I explained. "What you are hearing is from hidden speakers around the complex."

I laughed. "Welcome to what is called resort-style living. Its popping up all over these cities and each apartment complex has its own theme."

"Wow," she said again.

She raised an eyebrow and said, "At first glance it looks so real and impressive but it's all so artificial. These apartments are actually very small and wouldn't everyone be constantly bombarding each other with artificial frequencies from their phones and computers? How can they call this eco living?"

I laughed. "I have been asking myself the same thing since I arrived here a couple of weeks ago. At night I can hardly sleep, I am way too sensitive to all this EMF.

"Do you want to hear something really strange?"

She nodded.

"Would you believe that last night I saw a cloaked UFO come down over these very apartments and pulse certain frequencies through them while almost everyone was sleeping. I suggest they are using people's Wi-Fi and smart appliances to carry certain signals that alter our energetic bodies and dreaming patterns. They are seemingly doing this so they can collect our residual emotive energy as a sort of loosh for their own means and food."

"Wow," she said again a little more uncertain and questioning.

"You have always been a strange one!" she jested, however she knew of my extra-sensory abilities.

I replied, "What do you think my chances are of getting society to understand that we are being used and experimented upon by aliens and that these high and compact apartment buildings are really nothing but energy harvesting stations?"

She raised an eyebrow and said, "Good luck with that!"

Then I spoke in a more serious tone and pointed to the apartments around us. "All this so-called smart technology is very dangerous in the hands of our wayward leaders and governments. Can you feel where it is all heading?"

"Where are you going with this?" she looked at me.

I replied, "When you remove the palm trees, the colourful pool and the posters telling you that 'this is living', what do you see?"

"What do you mean?" she asked a little more confused.

"I am getting you to see that with one flick of a switch what people are calling secure and high living can become instant imprisonment."

She looked around at the tall clustered apartments, the security guards, high wire fencing and the many CCTV cameras.

"Wow," she said again.

She looked at me and her face was very troubled as we pondered together on the balcony.

THE LEFT-HAND PATH

When the truth is hard,
It is easy to blanket oneself in illusion.
When we refuse to face our pain,
It is easy to keep distracted.
When we don't want self-responsibility,
It is easy to just keep on going.
Shadows are an easy place to hide,
Who cares that the smiles are false
Or the air is poison.
Everyone knows, yet nobody admits.
There in the denial of Life,
It is very easy to blame others.
Yet as the light sears through the darkness
All will soon grieve and ask,
"How did we get here?"
But would I speak to you now
Of the Right Path to God,

Warren Sunkar

> You would just trample me to the ground
> As you run in the other direction.
> Too busy to care or to acknowledge
> Because it is easier...

RUNNING BACK UP THE MOUNTAIN

The golden rays of the Great Central Suns permeated all of God's creation.

Within the temple of Love and sitting by the side of his smiling master, Anura (whose name means regal heart) held alignment with the Source of All. Absorbed in infinite wonder, his golden robe of light shimmered fantastically as together they meditated on top of the Holy Mountain.

Here, Life's blessings were dispensed throughout the worlds.

One day as they were immersed in the great effulgence of cosmos, a strange murmuring arose from the valley below and upon hearing it Anura became distracted. As he attuned to these odd and discordant sounds he heard the cries and pains of many suffering beings and was disturbed as he pondered upon the chaos far below.

His master, sensing his disciple's distraction asked, "What ails you my son?"

Anura answered, "Master, this moment I find it hard to hold my alignment. As the cries of those in the valley meet my ears, it disturbs my being to know there is such suffering in those people upon the Earth."

"Oh them!" his master chuckled.

"What do you mean?" asked Anura.

His master looked at him and replied, "They are all suffering from a little lunacy."

His teacher then went cross-eyed and swirled a finger around his ear!

But his disciple did not understand this well intentioned candour and just frowned all the harder. Sometimes he did not understand his master's sense of humour.

His radiant master looked at him fondly and spoke.

"Here upon the mountain, we bring life to all of God's creation. If we neglect our duty then other worlds might suffer. Should those of the Earth seek their way out of the valley then nothing can truly stop them. They need only brave the mountain and thus we wait here to receive them."

"But master, no one comes!" Anura replied very seriously.

"It seems their cries are growing more desperate and I think it better if I went down to assist them. I will teach the way up the mountain to God. Nothing can deter me!"

The master looked into the eyes of his serious and grave disciple and he knew that look.

"I see you have made a choice and I know that nothing I can say will dissuade thee."

His teacher then stood up and walked over to a dimensional doorway on their left labelled 'The Shadowlands' and said: "The ways of this world are treacherous and dark, if the people see your radiance they will kill you. You will need to leave your golden robe here my son and put on worldly garb. Here in the holy temple I shall keep your golden robe and watch over thee."

Excited at the thought of helping humanity, Anura stripped off and put on a worldly robe. It had once been his master's robe long ago and had been saved for such an occasion. It was dull, colourless and very heavy but he would not let that deter him.

"God bless!" his master said as he opened the door.

Barely acknowledging his master, Anura did not see the tearful glint in his teacher's deep and knowing eyes, and with great enthusiasm and excitement he disappeared through the doorway to descend the mountain.

As he ran down the steep ravine he was so enthralled by his mission he hardly noticed the skies darkening with each step he took.

He pressed on down the mountain.

As Anura drew closer to the valley the air had become heavier and more polluted. The ethers felt lifeless and dense, and in a short while he realised he could no longer see the sun. He hesitated for a moment as the strange sensation of fear pulsed through him but then he pressed on because he would not let that deter him.

Then as Anura entered the Earth, strange sounds hurt his sensitive ears and there was an awful smell.

As he looked around he beheld many strange things.

Grey concrete monoliths towered over him through a polluted haze. Automobiles roared and beeped, unnatural lights flashed about him.

He paused to catch his breath. He felt queasy because the moon above him made him feel quite sick and disoriented.

Everywhere it was very busy and noisy and what was even stranger was Earth's humanity!

No one noticed him or each other. People would just walk by in a strange hypnotic trance. Their smiles had no joy; their movements were discordant with Life. Their eyes seemed vacant and they looked very sick yet they kept going about their business as if nothing was wrong.

Yes…Anura thought. Things were very strange down here!

He became confused and a little fearful because he did not know what to do.

Yet the fire of enthusiasm burned in his heart and he would have nothing deter him!

So he decided to stay for a while, trying to learn their language in the hope of communicating with the people.

He went to their schools of education and philosophy, watched their strange televisions and even frequented their very popular cafes. Yet over time, all this only confused him more because though they chattered a lot, they didn't seem to know what they were chattering about.

Their words were all nonsensical.

He felt a little sad and frustrated. So in an attempt to connect with Earth's humanity, he thought to imitate them for a while and began walking around in circles, smiling to them as if nothing was wrong.

In a short time the moon overhead began to completely disorient him. The heavy and polluted atmosphere began to make him tired and before long he fell asleep. In a strange state of dreaming he wandered around aimlessly with them.

Lost in this dreaming world, everyone was anxious and confused. The people did not realise they were asleep and they often argued with each other.

No one seemed to notice the strange black shadows that whispered incessantly into everyone's ear.

What was very strange was that everyone liked to wear heavy chains. In this dismal place the bigger the chains one had, the greater the social status. Some people wore chains so large and heavy that they could not move.

It was very surreal because everyone struggled so intensely under their burdens yet no one wanted to get rid of them. This was because in this dream world, great chains were high-class fashion and everyone who wore them thought themselves a king!

Everyone was quite crazy.

People wailed and howled, others cried or laughed manically as they worked so hard to get nowhere. Confusion pervaded everything and nothing made any sense. Everything was upside down and inside out.

It was complete lunacy!

Anura started to be overwhelmed with fear.

Then suddenly something fell from above and landed upon Anura's head, snapping him awake. He rubbed his sore head as he picked up a small stone. It was polished and its surfaces were reflective as a mirror. When he looked into it, catching a glint of light through the dark clouds above, he saw the smiling face of his beloved master and some words flashed through his mind… WAKE UP!

He looked around and wondered how long he had been asleep.

It seemed like lifetimes.

He remembered his divine mission – now nothing could deter him!

"Wake up!" he called to the people that walked about him.

But only a few of the people stirred and most of them just grumbled. They continued to go about their selfish business, bumping into each other, chattering incessantly and poisoning the Earth. They were all lost to their darkened dreaming.

Inspired, he thought to show them a better way.

So while they laboriously worked on meaningless things, he danced and sang before them.

They tried to ignore him.

As they bumped into and hurt each other, he would pick them up and heal them.

Yet they resented him.

He spoke to them about a Love that knows no bounds.

They grew suspicious.

Because he would not let them sleep, they grew angry.

Restless and disturbed in their slumber they began to circle Anura. Snarling, gossiping and threatening, he could hear the shadows in their dream world, whispering.

When Anura said he knew God, raising the mirror his master had given him to catch a small glint of light from the Great Divine Sun, they fell back, dazzled and confused. They called him evil; taking up their pitchforks and burning torches they attacked. Coming at him with a collective roar, they grabbed at his clothes and tore them off but Anura was light and swift of foot and jumped over them.

Naked, he took flight out of the valley. Like a comet, he tore up the side of the mountain as fast as his legs could carry him and nothing could deter him!

Nude and a little scared but with a sigh of relief he burst through the door into the master's temple. Panting and exhausted he looked up to see his master standing there with an expectant smile, holding his golden robes for him. Anura put them back on.

"What did you learn on Earth?" asked his master as together they sat down for a new planetary alignment.

Anura spoke thoughtfully: "One can offer the keys of Life but they will not free those who love their chains…"

His master smiled. "Anything else?"

Anura added, "Yeah! Before we can teach them about God…those guys will first need to learn a better sense of humour!"

(Anura went cross-eyed and swirled his finger.)

They gazed at each other fondly and chuckled intensely.

It was good to be home.

STRANGE TIMES

These are strange times, chaotic and unsure.
Smiling faces are the mask of a desperate and hidden war.
Rumours abound of an unearthly conspiracy,
Laughed at by the people as foolish absurdity.
Where evidence of deep state atrocity
Is covered up in disbelieving animosity.
Everyone is scared to admit to the truth
While poisoning the next generation's youth.

Those in denial all sing the same song.
Going about their lives like nothing is wrong.
But don't be fooled by this conflict of silence,
It is one of great inner violence.
People afraid to face what they must face,
Thinking their conscience can be erased.
A collective mind of this insane rationalism
Wear the jackboots of a new global authoritarianism.

Warren Sunkar

As those in high despotism
Seek to wield this growing fanaticism.
Sweeping us up into a fallen angel's spell,
Trying to pull us into their technocratic hell.
And while we observe this with great sadness
We shall not succumb to this growing madness.
Tempered and strong and with the eye of the soul,
We are breaking through all their mind control.

You needn't be afraid of what you see,
We are being called, to be set free.
Between the old and the new,
The many and the few,
Opens a growing rift
As the veils now lift.
Through the darkness shines a new light,
Revealing that which was hidden into plain sight.
And people are seeing what they didn't before
As the minds of the guilty try to conjure their war.

What we witness is not the end of Earth
But a new beginning, a planetary birth.
What is happening is beyond their comprehension
As we walk into a new dimension.
Beyond the limits of what they deem possible
We find ourselves realising the unfathomable.
These "End Times" are but the beginning for some,
Who aren't afraid to come undone.

A Little *More* Light From The Stars

Ignore dark whisperers and what they say,
We are rising to greet the new day.
As the shadows of yesterday disappear,
We shall know there is nothing to fear.
At the end of all that is history
Marks the unveiling of a great mystery.
As we stand to meet in the new vibration,
That brings us to true consciousness liberation.

ESOTERIC ARTICLES

AUTHOR'S NOTE

It is advised by the author of these works that the reader acquaint themselves with the first book of this series called *A Little Light From the Stars*.

Throughout these writings there is a differentiation between the use of the words 'alien' and 'extra-terrestrial'. The word 'Alien' is used in reference to those malevolent intelligences and beings whose origins are off-world and working against the divine plan for Earth. The word 'extra-terrestrial' is used to reference those higher and benevolent, non-terrestrial intelligences and beings, who are working in service and alignment as divine evolutionary forces for the divine benefit of humanity and the planet.

AN AWAKENING PLANET

At present this world is going through an advancing process of planetary rectification and ascension. Due to the aberrant conditions on Earth at this time, certain fail-safes have been triggered in the planetary Templar and now Earth and its humanity are undergoing radical change through a process of trans-dimensional shifts and interplaneal blending. With new subtle energies entering the earth as part of planetary healing processes, people and humanity at large are experiencing these planetary shifts both inwardly and outwardly and with a large variety of responses and reactions. There are a host of ascension symptoms that are displaying themselves throughout the collective, from physical maladies, psychoses and deep emotional catharsis to spontaneous awakening, multidimensional remembrance and the turning on of psychic and clairvoyant abilities. Some people are touching otherworldly realities, others feel time is speeding up and others just feel that the world is getting pretty weird.

Unfortunately, there is an extraordinary lack of preparation and understanding as to what is happening here on earth in regards to this cosmic event, with most of the populace unaware or oblivious to what truly is occurring. Earth is progressively shifting to its new station of identity within the inner planes of creation, and humanity, which shares a sympathetic multidimensional anatomy with the planetary structure, is also going through this catharsis. Whether we want it or not, our earth is going through these changes and so must we. It will be the choices that we make both individually and collectively that will define the nature of how we experience this time of fast changing realities.

With such lack of knowledge about the planetary situation, people are unable to intelligently respond to the changing landscape of human experience. With the rising challenges of today's world, many people are desperately and often subconsciously burying themselves in work, mundane pursuits and entertainment in attempts to relieve the inexplicable growing pressures they feel from without and also within. However, as the planetary tempo is raised, such shutting off will not assist people at this time and will in fact only lead to greater confusion and possible pain if people fail to recognise what is happening and begin to truly work together.

What humanity is increasingly experiencing whether they choose to deny these experiences or not is a shift into multidimensionality!

Shifting Into Multidimensionality

What is becoming obvious to many beings that are looking out over our mad and fast changing world is that we as a race desperately need to change the way we think!

It is inherently known that we can often limit our experiential possibilities in life through our perceptual filters and this is true on both individual and collective levels. Today, humanity's materially identified perceptions are severely hampering its ability to move healthily and coherently through current planetary transitions. Many people have many different perspectives of what is going on around them, and there is much confusion as to what is happening on the planet right now.

If we are to free ourselves and awaken with the planet, we must see that it is our temporal belief structures that often obscure or block us from seeing how things truly are. We must also acknowledge that most people have no real clue about how to resolve the world's growing issues and seemingly deteriorating realities.

Humanity can run on its delusions and denial for a while; however, this can be only for a short time. Eventually that which stops us from seeing the truth of certain happenings and matters must collapse in our changing and evolving realities, often to reveal the stark contrast and truth that we had been unable or unwilling to see for so long. This is what is taking place on earth at this time.

These writings are given to assist an awakening race through a tumultuous time of radical change and catharsis – to stimulate more questions so people seek deeper answers rather than take their lives at face value, to lubricate the consciousness and to get people to reflect upon why they are here.

A genuine approach and open sharing can evolve to right understanding and guidance which can often save people from much unnecessary pain. Let it be known that everything that one reads in these written pages has not come through conjecture or clicking through pages of media on the internet but has been earnt and learned through genuine real-time experience.

It's time to question everything.

So as we begin to explore the nature of what is happening around us, perhaps in the light of today's shifting realities, it is pertinent to ask oneself the following questions; If our modern materially identified society was forced to quickly shift its perception to perhaps embrace otherworldly realities or extra-terrestrial contact, what would the experience be like?

What new possibilities would open to us and what direction or course of action would our collective being take?

What would need to be re-assessed in terms of our belief structures, and what would be revealed around us that was previously hidden from our sight?

Laced throughout our modern and ancient cultures and religions are stories, myths and related experiences of other worlds, of angels, demons, avatars, ghosts, gods and things extra-terrestrial.

Often intellectuals and academics have written this off as superstitions or stories from a primitive past. But what if this is all part of our multidimensional experience and history which somehow and at some time we have forgotten or become disconnected from?

Throughout their lives many people have been fed Darwinian and Big Bang evolutionary theories, Newtonian physics, psychological and religious perspectives of our cosmos and journey on earth. There are thousands of theories, philosophies and speculations about our given reality that has shaped the modern schemata of the collective human mind.

However, today, many people in line with the planetary shifts are awakening their deeper intuitive faculties and experiencing shifts into higher stations of identity through which they can interface and assess their expanding sense of reality. They understand that the speculative human brain-mind is only a very small part of our full multidimensional anatomy and consciousness, and comprehends little of its surrounding reality.

As we awaken as a collective people we are seeing more and more holes in present day theories and are realising how little we know as a race. With new discoveries in science unearthing historical anomalies that challenge present day theories of history and changes happening within our multidimensional anatomy and DNA, we are learning through experience that all these intellectual and academic theories are only partial and often very distorted perspectives in comparison to the living moment of our current collective multidimensional awakening.

However, this is nothing new.

Mystery schools and divine masters throughout humanity's history always explained and taught perspectives of hidden history and subtle energy dynamics. They knew of our divine cosmic origins and the dynamics of initiation into higher stations of identity. They knew the power of thought and understood that our very belief systems can define or condition the experiencing of subtle realities and beings that unknowingly affect us and exist all around us. They spoke of contact and experiences with other worldly realities and taught about the responsibilities of right living. These have been largely ignored, shunned or forgotten by the collective and today many are paying dearly for this lack of insight.

As new Life energies continue to affect all life on earth, many people are awakening their higher sensory perceptions and are having many different types of unusual experiences that exist out of the current psychological framework. Sometimes this may be very confusing or frightening, especially for the unprepared. These experiences may be permanent shifts of consciousness or intermittent moments of lucidity or realisation; they may be flashes of past life or multi-dimensional recall or experiences such as extra-terrestrial contact. If people open up and are honest with each other they would know this phenomenon is increasing.

Unfortunately, we have been conditioned by modern society to often reject, laugh at or forget these transcendental moments as they flash through our lives. Unable to put them into a contextual framework within our current social and belief structures, we are taught to throw them to the fringes of perception, often treating them as strange, weird and unimportant. Yet, as we do awaken, we will come to understand that those often rejected and weird moments contain our true wealth and history.

Today, under divine cyclic cosmic injunction, new energies are radically changing everything we know or thought we knew. This writer would have people know that there is nothing to fear. We can work consciously with these powerful planetary and individual changes experiencing a more balanced and healthy shift. For some this will be a beautiful period of expansion and realisation but for those who are more resistant to change they might find the new earth terrain too much. But like it or not we will experience fundamental changes in how we both perceive and experience our given reality. Under cosmic impetus we are now being forced to change our ways.

Change has come...

So take the adventure.

We are called to become adaptive mariners in these new and changing seas throwing overboard those cumbersome and useless articles and weights that would hold us back. We must be cautious and conscious in this new terrain but not fear these changing realities in the knowing that within we have everything we need for this journey.

We must see the need to let go of our outdated beliefs, assumptions and learnings that no longer suit our new and rapidly expanding paradigm while at the same time rediscovering those immutable universal laws that we have perhaps lost or forgotten. We must now embrace a much larger framework of cosmic understanding.

THE NATURE OF CONTACT

Since modern humanity launched its first public space programmes, many people have speculated over the nature of contact with extra-terrestrial beings and other-worldly realities.

Throughout our known history, all cultures share their stories and myths of ghosts, nature spirits, orbs, gods and mystery.

Modern intellectuals and scientists might laugh at this but today, from their very own ranks, we are hearing testimony from some of the foremost experts in their fields attesting to extra-terrestrial contact.

With the expansion through the planet of certain natural medicines such as ayahuasca, tens of thousands of people each year are experiencing contact with nature spirits and other worldly beings and realities.

We have had presidents, astronauts, high government officials and military personnel coming forward with their experiences, and leaked classified government documents attesting to alien inter-relations often revealing that much has been hidden from the public.

People respect and even revere certain personalities and figureheads throughout ancient and modern history, but strangely, it has been the tendency to sweep their lucid testimony of other-worldly experiences under the carpet.

Today, many people have been going through an assortment of multidimensional experiences, and whether others have realised it or not, the world has already changed. With the ongoing processes of planetary healing, new energies are stimulating within members of the human race certain psychic and extrasensory abilities as well as their own multidimensional remembrance.

This writer has spoken to hundreds of them...

There are growing numbers of people who are also recalling their own extra-terrestrial origins as well as recognising that they had come to Earth to assist humanity and the planet in this time of change. These 'star-seeds' are remembering that they are part of a carefully orchestrated plan of assistance implemented from higher densities and spheres that have come to Earth as part of a greater plan of cosmic healing and rectification.

Many people are also understanding that there are certain less-than-benevolent beings that have come for selfish purposes of a more alien agenda of which we will reveal further in this book.

However, *all* of humanity over the coming period will begin to recognise that their origins and history are vastly different from what has been ascribed by our modern historians and intellectuals.

Such speculation as posited in this book might stimulate subconscious fears as programmed religious terror is invoked with warnings of demons, hell and damnation. This is unintelligent and will not serve us in the collective moment. Such bias is also curious because if people would look a little closer at the Bible and Scriptures they profess to study, they would see and understand that the texts they are reading are full of reference to contact with other-worldly beings and realities.

Somehow people gave up their own inner intuitive faculties, knowledge and insight to be replaced by external authorities who seem to talk a lot about certain subjects. However, with a little inquiry and probing, they seem to really not know much at all.

Or if they do, some of them have been purposely hiding it!

For certain people this book will stimulate a deeper curiosity, perhaps with a sense of wonder, remembrance and even expectation.

For others, this is nothing new. There is and has been a constant interplay with other-worldly realities and life forms.

There have also been many benevolent beings and servers of the race who have been trying to assist and guide humanity throughout the ages to these understandings and experiences. They were often ridiculed and attacked by a confused public.

However, no matter what our cherished beliefs are, we will all know that we are all constantly interacting with other life forms and realities.

It is understood by some that one definition for the word apocalypse means "the revealing". Much of what our modern humanity have deemed impossible, ludicrous and fantastic is now being unveiled as truth and people are realising that what they are now experiencing has always been there right before them, hidden in plain sight.

Contact has always been with us...

Our Expanding Sense of Reality

In the first book of this series, *A Little Light from the Stars*, I talked about the fall of humanity and how humankind through its misalignments unknowingly continues to shroud itself in a cloak of ever densifying and crystalising matter. We are coming to understand that modern humanity is in a very damaged state, and over time this has cut us off from being able to perceive or intelligently interact with the vast spectrums and dimensions of conscious intelligence that exist around us. We have become very limited to an extremely narrow bandwidth of consciousness perception.

As we proceed with these writings, people need to understand that it is sometimes very hard to relate to such a heavily programmed and materially identified race, the subtle nature of true and coherent multidimensional experience, and though many people have attested to actual physical contact with certain extra-terrestrial and alien beings, for the purpose of this book, it is more important to understand the multidimensional framework of reality we exist in. People need to realise that there are different grades and states of matter and spectrums of reality that we are constantly interplaying with even though we are not often aware of it.

As an earth shaman understands, a bird chirping sweetly outside a window, an insect in the room or a subtle breeze may have a lot more meaning than what most people would attribute to these events. Behind all of what we witness in this physical world are subtle forces and intelligences at play behind it.

Leaving our earthly relativities, what we see and measure through our telescopes and scientific equipment are but the effects of great and vast spectrums of cosmic intelligence that exist on multiple planes of existence. Modern humanity with its incomplete sciences, partial theories and crude material instruments has been mostly unable to accurately assess the true nature of our greater unseen realities that play within and around us.

Underestimated and drastically misunderstood by most, including scientists and the medical profession, are the possibilities of the physical body as an acute and powerful instrument of cosmic and subtle planes interfacing when in right relationship to its full multidimensional and subtle anatomy. When we are healed, integrated and clear, we can experience and interact with many dimensions of our universal reality and beyond, in the knowing and relationship of other and higher stations of identity that we can experience and work from.

In this understanding, we can have two people standing next to each other perceiving the same phenomena or event but with completely different levels and stations of awareness and relation. With relativity to our soul/spiritual realities, these greater heights of awareness come from stations of being that may be very far away from the linear brain-mind. That is why exchange and relation is sometimes so difficult with humanity who have tended to misunderstand and often ridicule anything beyond general mundane identifications and programmed consensus.

Expanding on this a little further, it is thus possible for two people to stand next to each other for a moment at a certain intersection of time/space but exist in different timelines or continua. At this momentary juncture on earth we have been experiencing this. We have been interacting, interfacing and sometimes colliding with many realities. Now as timelines bifurcate many beings are consciously transitioning into their new realities. This might seem a little strange to some but people often pass through different dimensions and reality frames without knowing it. Our ongoing awakening to new space-time dynamics and possibilities will be a very different experience indeed!

People observe and assess their reality through their awareness levels and belief structures as they experience it. Often these belief structures are usually contracts people share with others and society to reinforce a sense of control over their environments. This has always been a facade. Many tend to assume that the people around them share the same lineal constructs of reality as they do. This is definitely not the case!

With expanding awareness, people will realise that much of what is happening in the world today is not what it seems. Our multidimensional reality is very different to the mundane perspectives and storylines given to us by various media and academic institutions with many surprises yet to surface.

Humanity has relied too much on external authorities and physical instruments instead of its own intuitive faculties and knowing, and over time people's subtle senses have atrophied. However with new energies coming in, we are seeing a reclamation of these latent possibilities as more and more people are experiencing the subtle effects and nature of the planetary awakening. They are learning the nature of contact with other-worldly realities guided by their own intuitive and clairvoyant faculties.

As we awaken as a race it is important that we proceed attentively, carefully and with right intention. With depth of insight and clarity, we can determine the nature of contact with these other-worldly realities and beings. We are not helpless, and as people will learn we have many beautiful and powerful guides assisting us through this time of planetary awakening and healing.

However, we must be discerning as our galaxy and its races have taken some rather aberrant twists and turns. There are many different beings with many different motives and some are less than friendly. There are many experiences and dangers for the foolish and unprepared.

So we must also know ourselves better and more deeply understand the cosmic situation we find ourselves in. Whatever surprises appear over the coming years, know that we need not fear but instead embrace the expanding horizon of possibilities and potential. We just have to remember who and what we really are...

IT'S TIME TO MAKE OUR CHOICE

With the ongoing and intensifying planetary healing, many astute and aware beings are consciously experiencing multidimensional awakenings and shifts in line with planetary processes. As portions of humanity awaken to a more complex universal structure, they must now comprehend the larger nature of our given reality. As we step through into this new cosmic terrain, those on ascending pathways are finding that their new multidimensional configurations and bodies are perhaps more amazing, powerful and beautiful than they ever thought possible.

However, with the veils lifting revealing higher dimensional realities, there comes many new challenges and deeper understandings for all of humanity. There will be some powerful, beautiful and sometimes sorrowful realisations during the coming period and for this it is good to gain right perspective.

As we have been discussing in previous papers, humanity is experiencing more contact with other-worldly realities and beings. There are growing sightings and reports everywhere of extra-terrestrial and alien contact. However, this is often hidden or diverted from collective awareness through the mainstream media.

We hear names such as Lyran, Arcturian, Reptilian, Pleaidians, Greys, Draco and many more. Each race with its own diverse histories, experiences and agendas. Some are benevolent, others however are quite the opposite!

The author of this book has had numerous experiences and shared various forms of contact with many different beings and life forms over many years.

Today, as we come to terms with our changing landscape, people are awakening to the stark realisation that their given reality and present social structure is very different to what they previously perceived it to be. One of the more traumatic realisations that humankind will now abruptly face is that much of what people have thought life to be is almost completely opposite to what they have been told. While there have been many benevolent and beautiful beings trying to assist humankind over the last cycle, people are also awakening to the malevolent and very selfish nature of certain beings we share the cosmos with. We have often been played as pawns in a greater agenda as certain alien species have had a deep vested interest in Earth, humanity and what is going on at this time.

Today, as veils are lifted, many more people are questioning the nature of their existence on this planet because nothing is what it seems. As we wake up and step out into the multidimensional universe, people are understanding that Earth has become a veritable prison planet and in fact has been used as one for a very long time.

People are realising that some of those beings in power and authority in our given social structure are not who or what they pretend to be. Many have been working in compliance with certain alien species in an attempt to maintain their hidden levels of control and power. In their desperation to stop and distort the current planetary awakening, the world's controllers have launched a multifaceted attack on the human race and the planet in an attempt to subvert the whole human life field to their own miscreant ends.

There is a hidden war on the hearts, minds and soul of humanity to occultly enslave future generations of the race at this time.

However, before we touch a little more deeply on this nefarious multidimensional agenda, it is very pertinent to acknowledge that humanity itself has often hampered any attempts to assist the race.

It has been a sad fact that many divine servers have tried to assist humanity over the passing age and been rejected. Some, in the incarnational guise of divine masters, initiates, saints and innovators of their times, had sought to prepare a wayward humanity for this present time. They were often slandered, tortured and murdered by a wayward and misunderstanding humanity, and this continues today. Our race has made some very poor choices over past generations, and many people have known the direction our society was heading was wrong but have ignored the many warning signs given.

We are not powerless as a race, and with the right understanding and selfless action humanity can do much more to help itself at this time. It is living selfishly that we empower and attract those more nefarious and maligned entities and beings from the greater cosmos that seek to subvert the race to their own designs and involute pathways.

Even now in the face of total planetary destruction or worse, most people do not want to know anything that contradicts or contrasts their own self-centred agendas, relativities and perspectives. Thus humanity is easily manipulated, and many people are today falling into a pit of powerlessness, despair and confusion, seemingly unable to get off the designed treadmill of a very mundane and entropic existence and at the mercy of those who would use and abuse them to their own selfish ends.

Also it is important to understand that blame is futile, in the knowledge that humanity itself has contributed much to their agenda. Every time we act in discordance with what we deeply know as right and sell out to greed, personal comfort and selfishness, we fall deeper into the hands of despotic manipulators.

If you would deny this, then look around. How many people have stood by and done nothing while the earth is being raped, when reputable government and corporate whistle-blowers exposing inherent corruption and illegal activities have been persecuted, imprisoned and tortured? How many times do people mock and ridicule "conspiracy theorists" when most have been but genuine and simple people trying to relate their discoveries and experiences? How many times do people turn their backs on the blatant injustices of the world while trying to secure a strategic or monetary advantage over others?

Each time we act contrary to our true hearts and what we know is right, we set up circumstances that will cause us pain in the future. We do not get away with any misdeeds and eventually all that we have set in motion catches up and some of us choose to learn the hard way.

Telling your children that you love them and kissing them as you walk out to a job that is fast turning their world into a baron technocratic wasteland is a heated argument you will have with coming generations. One here would point out, that from a multidimensional perspective this argument will possibly be with your future selves.

These controlling and manipulative entities have required human hands and minds to further their agenda which humanity empowers through ignorance, greed and overriding its conscience. Look around at the state of the world – those who are not totally self-absorbed and can get off their mobile phones can see and feel that things have gone awry.

It is interesting that most of humanity would attribute to themselves an overdue sense of goodness when the state of the world reflects otherwise. Most people are inclined to selfishness, greed, illusion and thus darkness. What humanity is very good at is self-deception which opens itself to greater deceivers.

One here is not trying to browbeat anyone reading this work but trying to get people to take energetic and social responsibility. Humanity has opened the door wide to cosmic evil through generations of misdeeds and misalignment. People reading this piece might get upset and angry with what is said but in one's over-emotionality, such a person reveals the recognition of possible inherent truth even if they are trying desperately to deny it. That is why we must look within at our own motives before we can resolve the many issues and dramas within the world ego at this time. We will find that we have never been powerless but often mistaken as to what we have attributed power to be and to who or what we have given it away to.

For those in true knowing, authenticity has its own resonance so I need not explain too much about myself in writing this book. There is nothing to be self-gained from bringing this information to the public who often ridicule and attack similar works and their authors.

This writer has had attempts on his life on more than one occasion, has been harassed and slandered in the media and throughout certain new age circles, tortured, attacked and mocked. Has known friends and others die attempting to bring out similar themes throughout the world. All for the want and holding of a little truth!

This is the life of a true server of the race at this time on earth, and over the years I have connected and befriended quite a few. It seems some of us have needed to be put through all sorts of trials and experiences as part of the planetary healing and transmutation, and to gain a deeper perspective of what things are like and have been on earth.

Despite some of the harder and for some more frightening themes explained in these writings, it is important to see that this book comes as a message of true hope for humanity. Things are not always what they appear, and with the shifting and turnings of our awakening consciousness we will realise that there are always plays within plays. No matter what things seem like in this outer world, know we are in advancing stages of planetary healing and rectification. Humanity is reclaiming its inherent divine birthright. We are choosing our alignments and everyone is making decisions that will affect their future realities and incarnations.

Know this choice is yours and always has been...

OPENING OUR ANCIENT EYES

Today, we live in a time of fast shifting realities as humanity expands into a new paradigm of multidimensional awareness and meta-knowledge. As veils come off, humanity must fast adapt to this changing environment and embrace a much bigger and deeper cosmic perspective than what has previously been referenced. One of the deeper realisations that is now bubbling to the surface of the collective psyche is that we're not alone in this universe and in fact the universe is teeming with intelligent life!

As new energies enter into the planetary sphere affecting all of humanity, we are collectively going through a massive healing and catharsis. If we are to transition through these times healthily and sanely, we must intelligently acclimatise to this new terrain.

As we open to these changes we are coming to the remembrance of our ancient origins and purpose amongst the stars. However, with the current expansion of our earthly paradigm, people are also realising that humanity has and is being interfered with by certain malevolent alien species in an agenda to enslave the race.

Waking from the Dream

As we awaken to what has happened here on earth, perhaps we should first consider that most people look out at this world through their personal subjectivity. Such subjectivity is usually governed by one's personality identification, with one's perceptive lenses and filters influenced by many things including, environment, biology, genetics, health, education, culture, language, experiences and relationships through the span of one short lifetime. This personal relativism has us look into the outer world through our formulated belief structures and myopic assessments based upon what we have learned, our memories and associations of that which is usually personally affirmable or not. These perceptions and assumptions either obscure or enhance ones awareness and experiences of their given realities. This is what it means to be self-centred which is to be personality identified and currently 'human.'

Of course if we were a tree, our own relativism would be based upon our own experiences, capabilities and intelligence as a tree as to how we would interplay with and experience our given realities. Looking out into the world through its disconnected and separative nature, the human ego-mind can usually only speculate on such things. However, if humans were to somehow find energetic co-resonance with or become a tree we might be surprised at the living reality and intelligence of a tree and share the natural and empathic connection to our planetary intelligence that we have perhaps today forgotten. This would sound very strange to some but as shamans and esotericists around the world attest, this is possible. It is a sad fact that due to their self-centeredness, people and humanity at large often look out into the world through their disconnected relativity, experiencing their own distorted mirrors, dimmed by their own filters and are often highly inconsiderate to other perspectives, possibilities and experiences that do not fit into their personal assessments and judgements of reality.

The same could be said about possible intelligent life throughout our universe. We have often been fed, over generations, images of a seemingly remote or cold and lifeless cosmic reality and are told that somewhere out their life might exist. With the programmed ambiguity and illusiveness of deep space, we speculate into the known universe and often assume that we are the most intelligent life forms in the seemingly chaotic cosmos.

But what if that were not so and that all along it has been our own misalignments and identifications that have blinded us from seeing that which has been with us all along. Unbeknown and not usually considered by us is that our identification with the physical material world and reliance on the intellectual mind is but an inherent schism and defect passed on over generations through our very DNA that is blocking us from seeing that which is affecting us in every aspect of our lives… that our multidimensional universe is teeming with intelligent life!

At this point one might ask readers to consider, what would it be like to be an alien or extra-terrestrial? In consideration of our own limitations and relativities as a species, what if we had access to multidimensional perceptions and lived in other frequencies of realities? What would it be like if we had a deeper understanding of the mechanics, dynamics and history of the cosmos? What if we had much longer life spans than humanity, with greater abilities and technologies far removed from human comprehension? If we were benevolent, or malevolent, entities how would we relate and contact other beings of either higher or lower intelligence and how would we treat them?

Many people would think it foolish to even speculate on such things and therein lies one of society's many limitations.

However, as we as a race now awaken, many people are beginning to naturally shift their perspectives and relativities. We are now being impelled to adopt a more multidimensional perspective of our given reality. The veils are fast lifting and the world is fast changing and whether we like it or not things are not the same as they once were.

Of course it is all much more complex than this but this introduction serves as a simple platform to what is being implied in this piece. The point is that now in alignment with ongoing planetary shifts, humanity will shift beyond speculation and will now embrace the reality of extra-terrestrial and alien life.

Disclosure is here and now.

What is more, humanity is now awakening to its own history and part in this vast multidimensional cosmos. Our cosmic journey has been nothing like our current intellectuals ever thought possible, and our history is richer and vaster than what modern historians have perceived. We are understanding that our more ancient ancestors had far deeper knowledge of our planetary cycles and our collective journey through the universe. Some, in their wisdom, left certain clues and were even warning us about something.

We are awakening to the fact that certain malevolent entities are and have been working together for a very long time to secretly subvert the entire human life field to their own miscreant agenda. The design of which, is that much of humanity will be occultly enslaved to serve their selfish and despotic needs and ends for a very long time into the future.

Warren Sunkar

Seeing History with New Eyes

When we look back through our planetary history with eyes shaded by our own relative belief systems and experiences of modern life, we naturally distort and even completely obscure the truth and experiences of those times as they actually were. The tendency for modern humanity to think that it is at the current peak of its evolutionary processes is a mistaken tendency that limits its own ability to receive the wealth of experience, wisdom and information that comes from its true past. People assume that our ancestors were pretty much like us except a lot more primitive and without the technologies and understanding we have today. But what if that were not true? What if our reliance on our external material technologies, identification with material phenomena and our modern assumptions indicate a de-evolutionary and universally misaligned standpoint that we do not truly comprehend because we are closed off in a very damaged subjectivity?

Here it is also pertinent to ask; If certain hard historical evidences and proof have been discovered of knowledge and things transcendent or contrary to present belief structures, and if evidence of things has been given from our ancestors that are outside our collective assumptions and presumed possibilities, would we even be able to see or comprehend them?

A Little *More* Light From The Stars

The usual programme and tendency of modern humanity is to classify anything that is outside its given belief system or understandings as unimportant, obscure or even frightening. Sometimes something obvious could be right in front of us but we will miss it because it does not "compute".

It is also important to realise that this can also happen in any given moment when events or experiences from beyond our temporal view or understanding of reality are witnessed or experienced. The ego-mind, unable to coherently assimilate or relate to the experience, will often instantly forget, ignore – or in fear – deny or reject the experience. There are many scientific tests over the centuries documenting blind spots and weaknesses in the human psyche and ego.

In consideration of this, what if hidden alien intelligence understood our personal and collective psychological weaknesses better than what we do and have been exploiting our vulnerabilities and blind spots?

What advantage would they have if they knew our true cosmic origins in the multidimensional universe which we ourselves have lost or forgotten?

What if they had long ago infiltrated the higher echelons of our world social structure and certain government agencies and have been working from the shadows, controlling them for generations, in a coordinated attack against the human race?

What if they had removed most evidences and memory of our deeper and richer past, in a gradual takeover of the human race in which they had been shaping and moulding humanity over generations? What if our given history is nothing but a re-written artificial intelligence program inserted into our collective minds to obscure us from knowing the truth of who and what we are? Or if all that we think and have been told is mostly a lie and that we have been almost completely brainwashed!

Those who are awakening are realising that this is so.

An aspect of incrementalism that has been used as a tactic of warfare against the human race is that it is necessary to understand that humanity's current belief systems have been shaped over generations. Through divide and conquer strategies, mind control and social engineering, societies and peoples have and are being shifted from their inherent cultural/genetic memory and knowledge to forget their true past, to misleadingly embrace and assimilate an alien pathology that undermines their very connection to their cosmic and planetary environment as well as their true divine origins.

Let's say that over time certain elite in compliance with alien races have destroyed and distorted almost all records and memory of humanity's cosmic origins and vast multidimensional history in an attempt to control and steer humanity's future.

It seems that since a major invasion began back in the Sumerian/Egyptian period certain alien races have been increasingly tampering and interfering with human affairs and genetics. They have been purposely corrupting and destroying our subtle planetary grid, shutting down our interpersonal connections with our planetary mother and each other. Through this interference have we lost much of our collective racial memory and multidimensional perceptions, not even remembering that we had been taken over.

These alien species know that with the obscuring and falsification of our history, messing with our genetics and disconnecting us from our true divine origins, we become but corks floating in the great cosmic sea, without deeper purpose or true direction and are thus very easy to manipulate. With their greater understanding of cosmic realities, advanced technologies and advanced knowledge of time and space mechanics, these alien invaders have been attempting to subvert the entire collective human life field down artificial timelines and portals to achieve their own despotic ends.

However today, as we regain our true cosmic perspective and sight, we have the ability to penetrate through and beyond the generated illusions and glamour's of our mind controlled society. We are discovering almost nothing is what it seems, and today we witness a consistent assault upon humanity through various mediums and means of which most of the public are oblivious.

We are awakening to how much we are being tampered with.

The truth is that we have been living in mostly a manufactured and contrived version and distortion of our greater multidimensional reality. Much evidence of our planetary takeover and current subversion is hidden in plain sight but without the right context and understanding people are unable to see what they have been participating in and what is happening all around them.

It is this intentional generation of humanity's many delusions and illusions about the nature of their given reality that has given the ultimate cover for these manipulating entities who remain unknown and unseen, hidden and obscure.

However, under cosmic impetus this is now changing.

There will be many things in coming days that might seem confusing and even painful to digest for our awakening race. However, if we are to have a chance in these coming days and free ourselves, it might be wise to consider deeply what is being presented in these writings. Our Ancient Eyes are now opening, and in the light of what is revealing itself in these times we may have to give up many assumptions, learnings and comforts to navigate the now fast revealing spectrums of human experience.

However, know we do not have to fear what is being revealed from the dark cracks and crevices of this world. As we rise, we will understand our true capacity and strength to transcend the current prison matrix we exist in and escape the grasp of these cosmic predators. With truth comes deeper healing.

In the face of radical change and an unravelling into the new spiral of cosmic life, we are being called to leave our selfish and delusive realities and embrace the great opportunity that is now here. We are discovering that we have much help from those more benevolent guardians and races that we share the cosmos with if we truly desire to mend our errant ways.

Will we stand up and assume the self-responsibility that is needed as a race to embrace this moment of true consciousness liberation?

Time will tell...and the time is now!

COSMIC PARASITISM

If for a little while we would take a step back from our busy lives and take an objective look out over this poisoned and crippled world, what are we witnessing?

Our cities seen from above look like great circuit boards directing human energy to esoteric portals and power structures controlled by the elite. Our skies, land and water are becoming ever more polluted. We see in our fast dying oceans great oil rigs like mechanical mosquitos that are sapping the blood of the planetary mother. Mines like burrows penetrate the earth for its resources. Humans get up and go to their work in a spiritually somnambulistic state and no one cares about the damage they do.

This is parasitism.

Now through the advancing transhumanist agenda we see an accelerated infiltration in every part and function of our personal and collective being.

We are being bio/etherically implanted, mind controlled and augmented. We are giving more of our lives over to so-called smart technologies that are doing our thinking and work for us. We are interfacing with each other through artificial intelligence (AI) socially and now even sexually. We are being told by scientists and futurists that humanity's evolution lies in the merging of man and machine!

So what is really going on?

To understand what is happening to humanity it is important to know our deeper past. Here we go beyond the mundane perspectives of our modern academics to the clues left by humanity's ancestors.

In ancient literature and spiritual scriptures we hear of 'The Fall' where it is implied that certain angelic collectives and beings fell from their true cosmic alignment and connection. We are told that this collective alien awareness lost its way and became unable to receive energies direct from the God-Source, and over time became increasingly parasitic in nature. They began to manipulate, pervert and infringe on universal laws that govern our universal time matrix and then began to subvert or destroy other planetary systems and races, utilizing them to leech off their energy and absorb these worlds into their own aberrant false light structures. They thought to become gods of their own created worlds, and over time more and more of the universal structure became damaged and many realities and worlds were pulled into misaligned states.

As we awaken and come into a greater remembrance of our true divine origins and multidimensional history, we will also understand that Earth has been in a fall state with the rest of this galaxy, and remember that long ago our own planetary logos was infiltrated by some of these alien realities who have been manipulating humanity behind the scenes ever since.

Through this multidimensional fall from higher stations of reality and identity, humanity has engaged in ever more misaligned and corruptive states of being, to the point that our true cosmic origins have now mostly been forgotten and we have been very badly damaged. These alien species (called archons) have been silently using us as their food source, living off our energies that they siphon from us – even squeezing us when they need it. The true beauty and grandeur of our cosmic identity has been lost and our modern humanity has been reduced to the very limited material slaves we see today.

Hijacked!

Our universe is a conscious, intelligent and complex 15 dimensional structure and time matrix. It is made of a frequency spectrum and scale that is divided into an ascending/descending pattern of five sets of dimensional tri-woven reality fields of different density called harmonic universes. These in turn hold further sets of subharmonic frequency bands of dimensional scale. Within these sets of dimensional scale are the various stations of universal identity which our world and humanity experience and are past/future points of space-time location of consciousness identification. Our reality is holographic and we are at present existing in a world that has resided in the lowest harmonic, furthest from Source, that is evolving through an ascending dimensional reality and frequency spectra of light and sound.

Though time is simultaneous, as we descend into the lower vibrational fractions of dimensional scale from Source within this vast multidimensional structure, reality is broken down into various time-space pockets, or bubbles. These are kept separate by certain partiki phasing rhythms, different angles and rates of particle spin and energetic/time barriers that enable different and multiple vibrational realities to simultaneously exist without collision, interference or harm to each other. (Within all of this are numerous probability dominions and timelines that we can experience as we ascend through the scale of our 15 dimensional universal Time Matrix.)

Everything is intelligently coordinated and governed by divine and higher intelligence and regulated through time cycles. These cycles allow these barriers to open at certain junctures and alignments to descend and distribute certain energies between worlds, realities and dimensions thus enabling evolving planets and beings to accrete and ascend into higher frequencies and dimensions of reality. This is what is happening on our planet today.

However, over vast stretches of time throughout our cosmic structure, parts of our universal template became very badly damaged. These distortions created increasingly aberrant conditions and caused aspects of our universal reality to become cut off from Source. These manipulated sections of reality were unable to circulate eternal Life flows and were reversed and twisted into finite and artificial reality structures that progressively spawned many more misaligned beings, realities and worlds that are, and have been, interfering with our planet and many other planets within our greater cosmic reality.

Currently our world is in a time of ascension and at cosmic junctures – such as the one our planet is in at present, certain accesses are granted that permit communication, exchange and interchange between various and different intelligences, worlds, timelines and dimensional realities in line with karmic predispositions, alignments and the frequency-holding capacity of the ascending race or planet. In usual cases, this contact would be benevolent and expanding. However, with the periodic dissolution of these dimensional barriers and under certain conditions as we see in our damaged universal reality, our world can also be more vulnerable and susceptible to various cosmic entities and realities of a not-so-benevolent disposition and nature.

A Little More Light From The Stars

As many of these beings come from higher aspects of our universal structure, they have a deeper and more comprehensive knowledge of our universe than what humanity has retained, and are equipped with technologies and sciences seemingly far in advance of what our current humanity comprehends. This has made it very easy for them to manipulate humanity to their own ends, and by means of their artificial wormhole and cloaking technologies, these malevolent beings have been increasingly enabled to silently infiltrate our planet and accelerate their own personal and misguided agendas.

Unknown to most of humanity – particularly over the last few generations – these alien realities have duped certain governments and elite to participate in creating, opening, holding and manipulating certain organic and inorganic portals for them to proceed and progress their planetary takeover bid. Most of this has been achieved through secretive and various covert military operations and scientific experiments or projects at the heavy cost of the health and integrity of our planet and galactic structure.

This time of ascending realities has enabled so called 'intelligent exchange' between our world and certain alien entities to quietly progress without public knowledge. No matter what has been told to certain officials and shared between our worlds, the intent of these beings has been to merge, hybridise, capture and subvert our ascending Earth and its humanity at a very vulnerable time into their dying constructs of reality.

The Planetary Hacking

It is known that certain parasites infiltrate their victim to take control of their host's mind and often the victim is completely unaware that they have been taken over. They can do this by secretively and sympathetically taking over certain vital and cognitive processes, interrupting and co-opting the natural systemic signalling through which the parasitic entity takes over various functions and processes of its victim. We need to see this is as an actuality of what has happened and is still happening at the personal and collective level within our world today. Over many recent generations, we have been unknowingly witnessing an advancing strategy of replication, mimic and merger on every level of our personal and planetary reality to essentially take over and subvert our world as these fallen cosmic collectives drain and feed off our life force, possibly until our eventual consummation.

One of the aims of these alien collectives has been to run energetic reversals through our planetary structure and humanity to invert most of our reality and lock down our planet. They have been using their compliant elite for a long time, to shape and mould society and to control and run their anti-life structures. Humanity has been in a process of contrived collective subversion and thus itself is becoming ever more parasitic in nature. Today we see that another aim within the modern transhumanist movement is to get us to run AI signalling continually through our bodies as well as the planet. This will possibly completely disconnect us from our true divine alignment and organic matrix as malevolent forces use certain AI machinery to infiltrate, replicate and augment our world and merge humanity into their false light structures. They are blending us with their fallen artificial realities to trap our consciousness.

Understand, we are fast being harvested into an augmented and controlled virtual world.

Mixing and merging artificial and false light frequencies and sound with our organic spiritual matrix, re-encoding and then augmenting our reality, they have been attempting to seize and completely control the planet. Today, they are quickening their agendas and increasingly blending our organic reality with AI for collective consciousness transference. We are being completely taken over and our modern global society is being conditioned and manipulated to geo-engineer the earth while building its own technocratic prison. This has all been progressing aided and achieved by incessant mind control with its causes and true intent unknown and unacknowledged by most of the population.

All this they have been accomplishing through a process of negative entrainment, first gaining energetic co-resonance with their host through deceit and manipulation and then using mimic, theft and merger to secretively gain control over the planet and humanity to subdue it to their own design. Perverting, copying and simulating every inherent biological, mental, cultural, social and spiritual function to interfere with, capture, augment or reverse every organic human, planetary and cosmic process while remaining hidden in the shadows.

The nature of these cosmic predators is psychopathic with no remorse or care for the people they are enslaving or killing. Not unlike mad scientists, through their secret experimentation over the age, they have become well versed in humanity's vulnerabilities and weakness, and seek to exploit every opportunity they can with no care for the cost to humans or the planetary misery they create. This pathology has always been well exampled by their elitist minions throughout modern history, who have murdered and colonised their way around the planet.

When we understand the transhumanist agenda for what it is and why it is being pushed down our throats as our glorious future, we will realise that we are in fact experiencing an accelerated and heightened agenda of this alien infiltration.

Look at every single aspect of our lives and see the lie. Our sciences, religion, academia, entertainment, culture, biology, society and planetary systems are being increasingly AI dominated and infiltrated. We are told that our rising technocratic society is making our lives easier and better, while our planet is fast becoming polluted and uninhabitable. We are being told by certain thinkers and scientists that our evolutionary hopes lie in merging man and machine, and today we are being incessantly bombarded with this propaganda. All this is essentially a massive con with one aim which is to completely enslave us.

As we wake up, we will understand that other worlds and collectives in our universal reality have already succumbed to AI infiltration and we will discover that so called self-aware AI already exists. This alien reality is seeking to prolong its existence, and uses its methodical and systematic strategies – adapting to each world and reality – to capture and incorporate into its structure. Behind this technocratic prison we are building over ourselves, fallen metatronic consciousness is corrupting, absorbing and changing our planetary matrix to build a designed inorganic circuitry so that these fallen and wayward intelligences can simply plug in and gain complete control of humanity and the planet. We are to be used and exploited simply as an energetic resource.

It is important that people see the bigger picture of what is happening to humanity and the Earth today. We are being persuaded by certain authorities and media to increasingly open our biology to biohacking, experimentation and genetic modification. Our planet is now being blatantly geo-engineered. All around us we are ourselves building a prison of smart technologies while being told that they will make life easier and safer, when almost every single aspect of modern technological advancement that has become a mainstream reality is now being used to entrap us. They have been harnessing and streamlining our own creative capacities while manipulating us to enslave ourselves!

This alien strategy relies largely on their ability to keep us in ignorance of our divine nature and entire multidimensional structure, unaware of the universal laws that govern our true organic/spiritual matrix. This keeps us unable to correlate, comprehend and intelligently face what is happening to our world at this time.

As we continue to awaken and regain our multi-dimensional sight and abilities we will learn that we have the power and capacity to meet these seemingly overwhelming challenges. However, we must first come to more deeply understand the reality we exist within and be open to the growing possibility that our true universal structure is grander and more complex than what we have been led to believe. Then to truly face and resolve the many growing issues and drama of a hostile alien planetary takeover, we must gain a little more insight into how it has been happening!

THE ALIEN TAKEOVER BID

Considering a multiple species alien takeover, and in light of topics already presented in this book, it would be foolish to assume any takeover bid would be like anything humanity would expect or imagine. We have been constantly fed images and storylines by Hollywood, of great interstellar battles fought with lasers and spaceships, of humanity uniting and riding out to meet our intergalactic foes in triumphant battle. This is simply propaganda and part of the alien mind control program. The reality is very different as much of the real battle is hidden from sight.

It is no secret that leaked government documents have surfaced and that many people have come forward testifying to secret government programmes in which certain agencies and elite have been working in compliance with certain alien factions for generations. With the testimonies that have already been presented from various whistle-blowers and uncovered documents, it would be wise to assume these predatory alien species have more advanced technologies, weaponry, methods and means than what our race has acquired or understands. These aliens exist in higher dimensions of physicality, have longer life spans and deeper knowledge of our multidimensional cosmos. Having monitored and secretly experimented on humanity over generations, they have a deep understanding of human biology, psychology, energetics and sociology.

We are realising that we have already been infiltrated. In the words of esoteric writer Lisa Renee...

> *To be able to understand the sociopathic sick mind of Archontic deception systems, one would need to better understand the general attitude of an AD infected human or nonhuman (NAA) as having little to no remorse or empathy. If a technologically advanced extradimensional race has decided to implement a gradual takeover of a planet and its inhabitants, what kind of strategy would it use?*
>
> *First they would look to how they could maximize the efficiency of the invasion process and reduce the expenditure of resources that they have to generate themselves. To achieve this goal the secretive infiltration of the core societal organizational structures such as religious, medical, financial and legal systems, would be ideal to shape the value systems that generate reality belief systems they want to control. Through the engineering of a labyrinth of self-enforced enslavement policies based on fear and intimidation among earth*

> *inhabitants, they would achieve the use of minimal "off planet" resources by piggy backing on the earth-human resources. The people on earth would effectively enforce their own enslavement as well as enslave their own global human family by giving up their rights and resources. This is very effective for takeover and invasion with minimal resistance or revolt by inhabitants who are unaware they are being invaded. This is called the Archontic deception strategy. (LISA RENEE- ENERGETICSYNTHESIS.COM)*

For those with eyes to see, everywhere we look in today's society we are being pushed to accept a way of life that is alien. Over time we have been systematically disconnected and removed from our natural environments and are now being forced to embrace an artificial and technocratic reality that is devoid of true Life. We are being crafted through incessant mind control to accept values and belief systems that are in opposition to our inherent soul/spiritual nature. As we are conditioned to embrace these inversions and distortions of our collective reality it is we who are building our own technocratic-prison reality.

Today, the transhumanist agenda is fast being rolled out before us, and people are unknowingly being manipulated down timelines devoid of freedom and any form of self-determination. In the contrived labyrinth of modern life, people are being manipulated to remain blind, busy and self-focused, having little time or energy to question where we as a collective are heading.

One of the most important aspects of this agenda that some people are realising is that it has been imperative that these alien species have remained unknown and unseen. From the higher and hidden echelons or shadows of society and through their possessed and compliant minions in key positions of power in our hierarchical and wealth-based social structure, they have been shaping humanity's belief systems over generations. Over time they have infiltrated and gained control of every power based structure that runs our civilisation, and through manipulation of our information and educational systems – such as media, schools and religion – they have been able to control every facet and lesser structure of society. Our current social system has been engineered by a few in positions of wealth and power using deception, occult manipulation, mind control and force to create the inverse planetary structure of the new world order…that we see today.

It seems these alien races have been exchanging their technologies and knowledge with certain world controllers to keep them in power, and giving them life extension technologies and miscreant methods in diverting their karmic responsibilities in exchange for their compliance. Long ago these elitist bloodlines became self-serving, using perverted occult means and knowledge to keep hold of their power over the human race, and of late generations – in compliance with these fallen alien/angelic collectives – they have been mixing black magic with certain high sciences. Much of these hidden alien technologies are today being used against the human race in an effort to manipulate and damage us or to hide and distort the deeper knowledge and truths of our reality that we need to comprehend as a race to free ourselves. It seems our race has been bought and sold by the ruling class of our current society so that they may keep their positions of power and continue to abuse humanity for their own ends and self-gratification.

While these elite have been using their seemingly advanced but perverted knowledge to secure their dominance and power over humanity, they have been streamlining and compartmentalising mainstream science and education, keeping humanity dumb and in the dark. Manipulating our academia to embrace partial and hybridised sciences and theories that are sympathetic to their greater agenda, we often unknowingly use their self-serving and twisted knowledge in denial or disrespect of true universal law and greater reality. Today they are building our reliance on external technologies while hiding or destroying our true organic and spiritual potentialities.

We should understand that it is these fallen alien collectives which have been defining what it means to be human!

Warren Sunkar

We have spoken of how incrementalism is used as a way of shaping human belief systems over generations. It is also used as a warfare tactic by successively introducing different elements and advancing stages of their agenda, piece by piece, into many different countries and cultures throughout the world over many years. This has been one form of collective mind hack that infiltrates and acclimatises the world ego to unknowingly accept their agenda, while each country and culture embraces and unknowingly adapts to the silent takeover. This form of silent warfare and strategy is a way to keep people mostly unaware of the true intent of that which seems to be spontaneously happening around them, occurring as if by natural evolutionary processes.

However, today we see the archonic takeover bid is happening at an accelerated rate and now we are experiencing in many countries a more overt authoritarianism, forcing people to accept the many changes now being silently imposed on our unsuspecting societies.

During this time it is imperative that we as a collective are kept divided, confused and misinformed on many issues so that we are kept in ignorance of our true divine potentiality and running their gauntlet of mundane striving. We are constantly bombarded with useless and contradictory information, entertainment, sensationalist news and all sorts of distractions through various media.

Hidden factions in our own governments and military have been orchestrating terrorism and terror attacks so we are kept in an environment of fear keeping us in a state of perplexity and survival, unable to critically think and get the repose we need to understand what is truly happening.

Another common social engineering and mind control tactic is to use collective traumas and events – such as past wars, atrocities or mass terror attacks, most of which have been contrived – to take advantage of wounds and pains held in the collective human subconscious. In this way they exploit and excite the same repetitive reactions and responses of past patterns which they have studied and engineered as a means to further and hide their agenda. This is for the purpose of funnelling humanity into controlled outcomes and resolutions which certain forces harness as a means for further manipulation.

In this confusing, controlled and hostile social environment, they create a culture of denial and ridicule through academia and various media of anything that comes from outside official channels. Today, blind social conformity has itself become a culture amongst many of our youth. Incrementally over recent decades, they have infiltrated and effaced any true journalism and our mainstream news media has turned into a circus of disinformation, gossip and sheer intimidation. In such a contrived environment of chaos and fear everyone becomes scared of voicing – even admitting to themselves – what they truly sense or feel, and this is how people begin to feel powerless.

Our modern materialist society, through its conditioning, might find it very hard to accept the possibility that alien species could be controlling the race. Because of this, society can be easily manipulated to often join its very oppressors to attack and ridicule those who present rational evidence otherwise.

It is under this cover and hiding behind the power structures of society that these beings wage their war on humanity. Here they remain in the shadows and behind the shadows as the unseen manipulators of the great play.

The Greater Play

Until humanity itself awakens to and embraces its vast and greater cosmic heritage we will be unable to truly understand the deeper context of what is transpiring presently on earth. It is important to realise that the human race as we know it today, from a multidimensional perspective, is but a very sickened and sad remnant of what it once was. Through our fall from higher stations of identity, we lost much of our multidimensional capacity and have been reduced to a materially-identified people who have become a highly confused and dying race that has been stuck in an entropic reality of repeated reincarnation and misdirected purpose.

Our planet and its solar system have also suffered greatly due to the many aberrant conditions of our fallen universal reality and from hostile infiltration and experimentation by these misaligned alien realities. Unknown to most of present humanity, we are surrounded by off-planet machinery that has been interfering with Earth and severely damaging her connections to the greater cosmos. Our planetary mother, who has her own consciousness and journey, has been hijacked, raped and severely damaged, and often it is we who unknowingly participate in this madness. The deeper intent of certain miscreant intelligences had been that our planet and its humanity were to be slowly directed and drawn into the black hole at the centre of the galaxy which has been dominated and controlled by certain alien factions from what is known as the Yahweh/Abaddon Matrix.

Over recent years we have been experiencing an accelerated takeover bid because at this time of planetary ascension, these hostile alien species know that there is a chance that humanity and the planet could escape their grip completely and that they would lose their food source.

People are realising that the fast introduction of Wi-Fi telecommunications and their harmful EMF frequencies, genetically modified foods, pharmaceutical and chemical poisoning, food additives combined with certain external bio-modification and mind control technologies, are being used to damage us in a plan to inhibit our divine potential of true ascension. Today we are experiencing an attempt at forced and controlled bio-mutation and collective hybridisation by these alien factions – which are experimenting on humanity to keep their control – on a planetary scale.

In essence, humanity will discover that Earth has been caught in an artificial magnetic harness and was slowly being torn from its original organic cosmic matrix and alignment to be grafted to a fallen and artificial matrix to be slowly digested as food over time. It is through this artificial black hole portal at the centre of the Milky Way galaxy that several fallen races have sought to subdue and capture Earth and her humanity and why today they are striving incessantly to achieve their goal of planetary conquest. When we begin to see and understand clearly why these alien races are doing what they do, it becomes ever more obvious why we as a race are being channelled down certain pathways.

Today, we have reached a point in our collective processes that if we do not rectify our alignments, it will mean a very long and very hard collective journey back to our true divine source. If we are to be truly of service and true effectiveness in the coming days, we must first see that an alien takeover is actually happening!

Blinded and shut down, most people simply accept their given reality without questioning where they are headed or where society is going. While these alien beings remain in the shadows, people are unable to see how they are being programmed by incessant mind control through the media, religion and education. 'Life' goes on as normal as people in their amnesic daze go to work or play, reinforcing their programmed beliefs, giving their lives away to various social systems and structures to further the alien takeover of their planet.

However, with the global awakening that is happening at this time, some people are noticing that something is definitely not right with our current society. But unable or unwilling to get context of what is truly happening with and around them, many people, in fear, are clinging even tighter to their given social and belief structures as life is speeding up and seemingly becoming more chaotic around them.

As the tempo is raised, society is becoming increasingly destabilised and people who are unable to comprehend what is happening on earth are becoming more psychotic, confused and sick as they are unable to meet the demands of 'modern life'. This is because their misaligned lives are not being supported by those life-giving energies and benevolent intelligences that govern and work with our greater reality. Violent reactions and irrational tendencies are increasing and many people can fall into despair in a society that will not support each other through the current and ongoing shifts and awakening that is happening all around us. These archonic realities have been exasperating this collective confusion and psychosis, and out of this rising chaos, madness and possible war, we are being offered their solution and 'saviour' in artificial intelligence.

We need to work together in right context and with right understanding!

HOW WE ARE BEING USED TO ENSLAVE OURSELVES

We have briefly talked about certain historical events and the unveiling nature of our reality and the strange circumstances that we as a race are finding ourselves in – things that until now have gone on around us mostly unknown or unseen. There are many methods and means that the archons use to manipulate and enslave humanity and the planet, the scope of which is beyond this small book. Mostly these writings are but an affirmation and aid to others who have been going through various ascension processes, sharing this writer's own personal experiences and insight. To get a deeper understanding of this warfare being waged against the human race, one here highly recommends the works of Lisa Renee and African American Master Sadiki Bakari.

However, once again, I would like to point out that this writer does not shove all of humanity's problems and self-justifications onto 'aliens'. Much help has been afforded to our race, and our latter generations have made some interesting choices. Selling out what we know is right for personal gain always brings its consequences, and our lives that are played out on this earth often have the interesting quality of reflecting back that which we don't want to see about ourselves.

For instance, we gasp in horror at the thought of an alien species experimenting and feeding on us yet do not blink when we eat a steak or use animals for science or product testing.

We might get angry with the understanding of a so-called 'illuminati' trying to control and dominate our lives yet often we do not want to take true responsibility for how we should ethically live on our planet.

We might get frightened when considering that we might now be ejected from the planet and removed from our current evolutionary stream into an artificial prison reality. However, many people often turn their backs on truth and what is right because it has been easier to live in one's illusions.

Perhaps we are learning a deeper lesson. We have a true evolutionary option if we want to hear it and reclaim our energetic responsibility and planetary stewardship. A lesson reflecting what we have become and what we will become if we don't fast mend and change our errant ways.

However, this is true only to a point and it is also important to recognise that these archonic realities have consistently overstepped and infringed upon the boundaries and rights of many worlds and beings.

This writer has also observed a vast array of technologies and subtle weaponry now being secretly used against the human race, some of which includes various frequency weapons and devices, bio-etheric implants, holographic inserts, mind wiping devices and etheric weaponry/splitter tech. We are being poisoned and/or genetically altered through chemtrails, pharmaceuticals and our food and water. We are being mind controlled through the mainstream media, education systems, religion and Hollywood via incessant propaganda and subliminal techniques. These miscreant intelligences are destroying our inherent spiritual values while they mainstream Luciferianism and Satanism to indoctrinate us into a death culture of anti-life values.

Humanity is over run and overburdened, and it is this continual, abhorrent abuse which has called upon the current divine intervention of which we will reveal more in later writings.

Though most of humanity has consistently ignored the many warnings afforded to the race by its true servers, people today still have the opportunity and choice of where they put their alignments. Under universal law we are held responsible and accountable for our choices and the actions we consciously take. Wilful ignorance can also be a choice and has its repercussions. That is why it is pertinent to comprehend that we must see clearly how we, ourselves, are being used to further the alien agenda so we can choose alignments to our possible future destiny.

Our Illusions Imprison Us

It has been said that one of the primary means of the planetary takeover is that we are unknowingly conscripted in a war against ourselves. This has been done through mind control and social engineering while humanity's true oppressors remain unknown or hidden in the shadows. Using their compliant elite minions and people who sell their souls for personal wealth, power and gratification, they have embedded themselves in the power structures of our global society to maintain their control and either knowingly or unknowingly, effect the greater planetary subversion and takeover.

It has been mentioned in these writings that one of the main objectives of the alien takeover strategy has been to run energetic reversals through the planet and humanity that feed into anti-life structures while running AI signals through our bodies. Over time, this disconnects and completely inverts people's reality, keeping them unable to embody their divine and higher stations of identity. All the while they are continually inserting belief systems of inversion and distortion through their incessant mind control and subtle technologies. Our entire global civilisation is now an engineered portal through which they harvest and utilise our energy and energetic by-products to feed and maintain themselves and their greater off-world artificial reality structures.

In this state of collective inversion, almost everything in our society runs involute to what it professes and actually should be. Thus our media misinforms us, our medical profession poisons us, our legal system supports chaos, our religions spiritually imprison us, our defence forces are used against their own people and the list goes on. Every day we, the people, support these anti-life structures by going to work, reading the newspaper and just following the 'programme'.

Over time our culture has become extremely toxic and we have been led into a global death culture that is fast losing any true soul values and which has become a breeding ground for psychopathy, sickness and energetic vampirism.

Today, what most people consider to be normal behaviour only reflects society's degeneration. True environmental considerations and self-responsibility are being forgotten while the people are implanted with ludicrous or superficial ideals such as fighting global warming through taxing or getting rid of plastic straws and shopping bags. The shallow and unthinking do not see how such 'solutions' are merely Band-Aids and are purposeful distractions while true social conscience and living ethics are being deliberately erased. Under the 'New World Order', blind social conformity is what people demand and it dictates almost all of what people say and do.

Another example of the many 'solutions' of today's degenerating society is that over the last decades people are being increasingly regulated by pharmaceuticals. This writer has spoken to policemen, teachers, army personnel, politicians and others in positions of responsibility who have been on or are taking various anti-depressants or anti-psychotics. These are the signs of the deep and inherent sickness of today's society, indicating misalignment with life. How can people expect to effectively raise coming generations when their very peers are unable to deal with or understand the real conditions on earth at this time? No one speaks about this because it is so widespread and endemic. This is how a planetary hell is created.

Now we are being mind controlled to think advancing AI technologies are our planetary saviour while being conditioned to see those who would harm us as our hero or problem solvers. In truth we have even become so brainwashed that we love the means and technology of our own enslavement. Know that technologies such as your iPads, smartphones, computers, cell phone towers, robots, smart and wireless technologies have been weaponised against you.

Through incessant propaganda, those in power are consistently trying to override people's own inherent and critical thinking capacity, to try to delude us that our world will get better with AI. They are constantly trying to beat out that we are evolving through our growing technocratic reality and this might seem true for the superficial or brainwashed but with a little rationalisation and depth in thinking, the opposite will reveal itself to be what is truly happening. Those who have thus lost their inherent soul alignment and intelligence are unable to understand what is taking place and will embrace these programs and illusions to become the builders and keepers of humanity's self-perpetuated prison.

These archonic intelligences are very versed in exploiting our weaknesses and use illusion, glamour and Maya to manipulate and entrap us by playing upon the primary fears of the personality. They do this by stimulating and controlling our egoic tendencies for survival, pleasure and vanity, (in short our selfishness) to have us continually invest our time and energy into their inverse and finite structures, constantly chasing temporal manifestations while creating karma through our energetic connections. This keeps us on an incarnational treadmill into these lower realms which today they are completely hijacking.

Look around and there are many different 'things' to lose oneself in today – work, computer games, Hollywood, music, shopping malls, the list goes on and all are increasingly AI dominated. We are increasingly living in a world of cloned realities and culture, all of which are completely unsustainable environmentally and come at the cost of our collective sanity. Our children are caught in a whirlpool of gaming addiction and AI possession.

While the growing technocratic infrastructure is promoted as making our lives easier and better, this is simply a lie and is only about short-term gratification at the immense cost of future generations. People are easy to train and often willing to seek self-convenience over what they know is inherently right and have been selling out to this everywhere.

Today's society worships wealth-based structures and capitalist values in which people emulate the so-called wealthy, famous and powerful. Many have been taught to view this as 'success'. People have acquainted acquired wealth with intelligence when this is simply not the case. For those with the eyes to see, they can observe the immense cost that misappropriated wealth, fame and 'power' is having on humanity and the planet.

As new Life energies enter the planet, people will now awaken to what they have been supporting. At the core of our global social structure is a cabal of Luciferian and Satanist groups, hiding behind and controlling our society. Today as certain veils of consciousness are being removed, people are seeing the atrocities of satanic ritual abuse that lie behind much of Hollywood, large corporations, mainstream religion, politics, royalty and other power-based structures.

To capitalise, today, means mostly to exploit and get as much as one can usually from human, planetary or off-world resources. A capitalist culture merely promotes selfishness and greed throughout our world and only empowers those world controllers who sit in the higher echelons of our inverted and materialistically inclined society. Until we stop venerating our illusions and re-think the cost of our global society's very warped materialistic value system, people will continue down these degenerating pathways, possibly to their doom.

There is a very high cost in selfish attitudes and living because it only disempowers us. It often gives us the illusion that we are 'getting ahead' and this might seem true for those who are self-centred and materialistically inclined but in reality it is usually at the expense of others or our Earth while collectively we are fast pulling each other down a cosmic sinkhole. Selfish attitudes and greed destroy our empathic connections to Earth and each other, drastically limit our scope and awareness of our greater multidimensional reality and thus we are easily controlled and manipulated. Understand that it is *we* who have been mostly used to suppress and fight each other and build the infrastructure of our fast growing technocratic global prison system.

Building Our Own Global Prison

Over the last decades this writer has travelled through many countries, particularly in South-East Asia, where in some countries the AI agenda has been advancing more rapidly than most. (Observing many changes and watching the fast encroachment of biometrics, CCTV cameras and smart technologies.)

New housing developments and 'smart' living estates in Asia openly cultivate an attitude of superior living. They boast boutique shopping malls, entertainment facilities, higher security and cleaner living standards when compared to the many downtrodden and poorer areas around them. But these developments are nothing but the manicured face and foundation stones of the new high-tech, global planetary prison system. Few people consider that through a premise of 'secure living', technologies such as biometrics, smart technologies and Wi-Fi will easily be turned around and used on multiple levels to imprison them.

Introduced into some Asian societies and now slowly into the West, has been the advent of social crediting systems. People are rewarded with social credits should they do what is officially sanctioned or approved by their government, such as going to government approved events, visiting government approved websites and working hard in certain jobs. This enables people to have certain social rights and privileges while 'discrediting' those who choose other options. This is blatant mind control and social engineering.

Oops, this writer may have just said too much and lost his access to those smart public toilets in China!

Should people think a little of the possible misapplications and uses of smart technologies by an authoritarian government and system they would be horrified. How far away do people think it is before those discredited people are targeted for 'legal' killing, torture, imprisonment or sanctioned brainwashing?

In fact, in certain countries, this is already happening!

I recently visited a small South-East Asian country that is perhaps more advanced than most in the AI agenda. In this country everything is monitored by CCTV cameras, facial recognition software and smart technologies. There is almost nowhere anyone can go without being monitored or assessed. In this country, trees also have cameras hidden on them!

People live in small flats and 'smart' apartment buildings, many of which have biometric security. Due to high density and expensive living conditions, everyone is constantly working and most of the small amount of leisure time they are afforded is mostly through AI.

As one of the more aware citizens explained to me;

> *A few of us now understand we live in a totally controlled society. We are constantly monitored and people are too afraid to speak out. Protests have become almost impossible because of all this surveillance technology and are stopped before they can even be started. Now people are being put in jail for just speaking out against the government. The media says nothing. I was speaking on social media*

> *to my friends about this when I was interrupted and warned by a government authority and told to be quiet or face harsh consequences. This is unbelievable!*
>
> *If we get caught talking to tourists like I am now, my license which I need to work will get revoked, we have to be very careful. Tourists and visitors to our country are completely unaware of what is now happening here, they come here because it is 'safer and cleaner' than other Asian countries. But they do not understand and mostly don't want to know.*
>
> *"Now the price of fuel and food are about to double. No one can afford this. We are slowly being worked into the ground and we find ourselves helpless."*

In these countries people are awakening to a technocratic nightmare. In certain countries people are now being threatened by government and law enforcement personnel for sharing anything on social media or the internet conceived or deemed outside mainstream interest or government approval. More and more people are being thrown into prison for just speaking out against the government and its often corrupt practices. This is a current reality and not 'conspiracy theory'!

On the surface, these developing hi-tech cities seem cleaner, glossier and friendlier than other parts of Asia. But mostly this is just a contrived illusion of a social environment of psychological oppression, and many people are living in fear. In many Western countries we are seeing the same patterning and blueprints being introduced into our own cities and it will not be long before we find ourselves in the same situation.

We must see the bigger picture and global patterning of what is actually taking place today in the understanding that it is we who are building a global prison system around ourselves. People should ask: What is all this saying about ourselves?

We should not be afraid to ask ourselves and each other the hard questions...

A SILENT WAR

It has been written in earlier sections of this book that a war with alien realities will be unlike anything we can expect or conceive and so it is. Today, humanity is under an accelerated agenda to counter our current global awakening through artificial intelligence technologies and weaponry that are being used by certain alien factions and government agencies to further their takeover agenda. We are being secretly attacked on every level and in every aspect of our lives – personally, collectively and multidimensionally – a silent and mostly invisible war that relies on mind control and advanced technology to manipulate and damage humanity and to recruit us as our own captors.

With much of humanity still mostly unaware as to what is taking place, we need to break this spell of secrecy and silence. It is for this reason that this small book has been written.

Today, the more astute people have become aware of the great arsenal of technologies and weapons that have been developed and amassed by certain

A Little *More* Light From The Stars

governments and covert military groups. Some of these include plasma weaponry, weather changing technology, cybernetics, germ-warfare, holographic technology, drones, robots and more.

While some of this weaponry is publicly known, much of it is still only speculative in public perception. However, with just a little careful discernment and personal research, it does not take long to realise that those in power have many interesting and incredible technologies at their disposal. Yet all this, it seems, is only the tip of the iceberg. There are many weapons and technologies that the general population is mostly unaware of.

In regards to the war being waged upon humanity at this time, people need to quickly face the reality of frequency weaponry and understand that these technologies are being currently used against the race all the time and for all sorts of reasons. Frequency weaponry is used by certain groups and agencies because they are much less visible than known conventional weapons and often come under the guise of silent, slow-kill or soft-kill technologies. They have many applications, and these weapons are easily disguised. Unknown and undetected by people, they can strike individuals, groups or nations, from near or afar, with their victims usually unaware of what is happening.

Today, they are secretly used against the public to make people physically and mentally sick. They can target people's physical and subtle bodies to damage or alter their minds, energy fields and DNA. They can be sent directly into people's brains to alter perceptions, wipe their minds and rewrite their memories; they can be used to drive intended victims to insanity or suicide and are employed for direct assassination and murder. Frequency weapons are much harder to identify as murder weapons because they often don't leave the usual markings of more conventional weapons and can be confused with various terminal illnesses and diseases, organ failure or insanity.

They can come in many forms, from high-tech military hardware to much less obvious household appliances. People are realising that elite-controlled government agencies in association with certain corporations, have been weaponising cell phone towers as well as computers, mobile phones, televisions and many other modern household appliances termed 'smart technologies'. It is recognised by more and more people that many mainstream technologies have multiple hidden applications and 'back doors' through which certain secretive government agencies or corporate entities can use to spy on people. Even though governments and corporations denied it for many years, it is today proven that these household and personal technologies are being used to constantly gather personal data and information and to monitor and track people.

While people have obsessed over obtaining the latest iPhone, or programmed to demand faster and more powerful internet, in just a few short decades the public themselves have unknowingly funded and assisted these corporations to build their weaponised global infrastructure by buying and placing most of the military hardware in their own homes. The deception lies in that if people themselves are doing the work for these corporations and purchasing the technologies themselves, they are a lot less likely to believe such a conspiracy exists.

However, testimonies from credible people in government and military have disclosed the reality of various frequency weaponry and that these hostile technologies are being used against the public and tested on small populations in secret.

Even if we were to remove the 'alien factor' from what is being discussed here, when we see the fast rising telecommunications network and artificial EMF frequency matrix that is rapidly encompassing our planet, we are handing certain elite and governments virtually unlimited control over our lives.

This writer would posit the question: If history has shown us that despots have always risen to power and abused it, why would we grant such power to those in control today?

Warren Sunkar

The Propaganda Campaign

Over the last couple of decades, various speakers, writers and thinkers have been laughed at, ridiculed and attacked for presenting or explaining the many problems and themes that have become a reality today. Many sound and coherent people were labelled idiots, conspiracy theorists or crazy and were shunned and disrespected by the public themselves, who have been easily manipulated to turn on each other rather than question what actually has been happening in the higher echelons of our global society and all around them. This was by design and it has allowed those elite and governments to get away with murder. It has also given them time to streamline the population down certain pathways and condition them to accept that which was unbelievable in the past, through their incremental warfare strategies.

This harassment of free thinking continues today, and society has been crafted in such a way to reject anything that has not been given to them by government, corporate-sanctioned authorities or mainstream sources. *This is mind control* and is easily recognised when people disregard or do not acknowledge credible evidence and proof that may be contrary to their personal beliefs or that which has been deemed socially acceptable.

If people would take a step back from their busy lives they would understand that we have witnessed a change into a more centralised global authoritarian structure with most of the world's population unable or unwilling to see what has happened. It is imperative to recognise that certain government groups and elite have indeed accomplished much of what certain 'conspiracy theorists' were propositioning only decades ago. Look around – most people have already come to accept the technologies of their enslavement. In most countries group think and government enforcement is fast replacing any remaining individual autonomy, while anyone questioning or vocalising against the current collective trends and programmed mindset is still being ridiculed, shunned or worse.

Over the last decade many whistle-blowers have come forward, and credible documents have surfaced revealing the appalling truths of what has been going on within our governments and behind the closed doors of our elite corporate structures. There are countless scandals coming into the public domain and many lawsuits are being filed all around the world at this time. It is very easy to see that corruption has become endemic within most countries' governments, and though many politicians don't know the deeper alien agenda, many high ranking officials have been bought and sold. We must understand that we are facing liars, abusers and cheats who hide behind their self-made rules and laws. We can see how the term 'national security' has often been invoked to hide much of their criminal activity.

In light of our recent past, people can now recognise how they have been duped. In regards to many of these high elite and government officials, any outward show of care for humanity or true environmental concern is but a simple façade. We hear government pledges of "fighting global warming, global poverty" or "the war on terror" but these are just lies told to gullible populations. These are usually either distractions or emotive plays that use the public to unknowingly assist their globalisation agenda, to enforce their laws and build their global prison system.

As part of a collective mind-control programme implemented by those in power, we have been witnessing over recent decades complete government infiltration and takeover of all forms of media. This is blatant authoritarianism and there is now unprecedented censorship on whistle-blowers for exposing the many corrupt and criminal dealings we see around the world today. People are being harassed, imprisoned and killed for coming forward and doing the right thing, while the corporate mainstream media is used to attack, ridicule and ostracise anyone not in compliance with the takeover agenda.

Over past decades there has been much fabrication or semi-fabrication of mainstream news and information, while attacking any true alternate views and facts that rise counter to 'official storylines'. We are witnessing constant and incessant propaganda for various elite sub-agendas and manipulation of public opinion, on screen and through our newspapers. This is also done through online social media, with many government and corporate implants and imposters used to harass or confuse the people.

There have been both staged terror events and actual terror attacks which are part of a social conditioning strategy waged in high-tech mind warfare against our global population. The various methods and means certain elite have been using to control the race are many and multiform.

All of this is now being used to confuse, control and subdue the general public.

Know it is never wrong to question and hold to account those who are in authority, and in fact it is *our* responsibility to do so if we want a free and open society. Governments need to be more transparent and to discuss openly where we as a society are headed and the reasons why.

The Transhumanist Agenda

As we come to the inevitable realisation that despite decades of public disbelief in regards to the elite new world order agenda, much of what was laughed at and ridiculed only decades ago has already manifested as a global reality. With the advantage of hindsight, we can more easily trace back how certain elite strategies have been implemented over the years and how the general population were themselves used to further this agenda. By looking back we are able to see with greater clarity how we have been manipulated, and it helps us to be more conscious of where we will put our energies and alignments in the future. It will also give us greater insight as to where these elites are presently directing us.

In the first book of this series, *A Little Light from the Stars*, we briefly talked about the alien-led transhumanist agenda and how we are being manipulated into accepting a way of life that is inverse and anti our true soul nature. With what has been revealed thus far, in these more current writings, it is pertinent to expand on this agenda a little further.

Over decades and despite many warnings to change our ways, people have participated in the incremental destruction and geo-engineering of Earth. While the true regenerative potential of our planetary ascension processes have been hidden, people have been conditioned by a multi-generational propaganda campaign to manipulate and force them to increasingly integrate certain artificial intelligence technologies into their lives. Instead of coming into deeper knowledge of their true organic/spiritual potentialities, people have become ever more reliant on external technologies and AI to do much of their thinking and work for them. We are becoming increasingly removed and detached from our natural environments and pulled into an inorganic reality as our true spiritual foundations are being attacked and eroded.

Think about it!

We are witness to a massive propaganda campaign over the last decade to get us to accept robotics, virtual reality and cybernetics into our lives without any true debate as to the environmental, psychological and spiritual costs to ourselves and the planet. We have been groomed over decades through our television to accept transhumanist themes and reality. If a person has the time, they can see in many older television series, movies and advertisements over the decades, obvious subliminal and overt inserts and programs that have been fed into the collective subconscious through their incremental warfare strategies. Through mind control and emotive conditioning, these elites have been steering the collective down transhumanist pathways with very few people understanding what has been happening. Not only does this suggest the complicity of Hollywood but also indicates deep pre-meditation.

Today we are also able to see the drastic effect it has had on the younger generations who can tell you more 'facts' about Pokémon or the Marvel Universe than about Earth, ascension and the multidimensional universe around us. People are now spending more time online than gaining essential life experiences and are relying increasingly on various technologies to do the thinking for them.

It is important to understand how we are being manipulated to give our lives over to AI. We are being slowly dumbed down, dehumanised and degraded in every way possible, while robots on screen are seemingly becoming more aware, amazing, human and empathic. AI is extending its loving hands to help a lost and doomed humanity, and in their desperation and confusion many people are buying into it.

These programs or *enchantments* would have us believe that heroic cyborgs will still possess a high degree of freedom and individual autonomy, or that artificial intelligence would care for humans. Nobody questions why robots are given human, semi-human or cute animal features in many Hollywood movies. This is intentionally appealing to our hearts through emotive reflex and associative conditioning, when in reality AI would copy and embody more efficient bodily forms as a higher and more efficient means of work and production, which, in our current 3D reality, should probably resemble more of the insect realm.

But maybe to humans in their present state, wouldn't that seem a little less appealing?

We are increasingly being fed themes of how many of these new technologies will save us, and today we see the transhumanism movement attempting to roll out much of its agenda through salvic environmental themes and healing technologies. As the agenda advances, many of the new and coming technologies that are to be released might seem simply miraculous to many. They will be able to seemingly clear our polluted lakes and air, repair or heal our physical bodies, perhaps even remove nuclear waste, all the while making our lives seemingly easier. However, this is but a ruse and hides its true environmental, psychological and spiritual cost. Much of the nanotechnology that is being developed today is secretly designed to infiltrate and infect all biological systems, to change and interfere with our inter-cellular communication and DNA signalling. The aim is to take over our natural cellular and systemic functioning, while they offer their inorganic and synthetic solutions to gain further control over the planet and our personal biology.

And there is more...

It is today understood by many more people that secret deals have been made between certain governments and alien groups that have shared and exchanged information and technologies with most of it hidden from the public. Yet few people understand, even amongst government agencies themselves, that these hybrid technologies are in fact compatible and are able to be used and controlled by more advanced alien technologies from other dimensional levels and realities. It is these alien groups that will remain in control and can easily override these existing technologies for their own deeper agendas.

With many more people multidimensionally awakening, they are coming to better understand the greater complexity and multidimensional drama that we are in fact facing. Hidden alien technologies are a reality and are being used to target both Earth and its populations in various ways. Those who have regained their multidimensional sight know that our subtle bodies are being infiltrated with various AI implants and technology that utilise, distort and affect our light bodies and cognitive processes.

Few people consider that certain AI frequencies can also be used as carrier and transmitting waves for certain intelligences to implant or possess beings, or that people can be secretively altered and programmed to commit crimes and acts of violence. This technology exists and is being used, and some of those random killings or brutalities that make headlines in the newspapers are in fact AI possession.

More people will start to understand that there are individuals hidden in certain positions of our global society who act as portals to alien artificial intelligence, who have been manipulating and shifting all facets of society to embrace certain transhumanist themes. Few people yet understand to what extent this has been happening but it is now becoming increasingly suspected. This is not written to create animosity or fear but to have people understand the complexities of what we are facing.

Now we are being told by our mainstream media that our world is soon to be blanketed in AI frequencies and signalling, which will create a 'new world' of heightened interaction and possibility. This has come at the literal crux of our collective organic ascension into higher stations of identity and awakening multidimensional potential, offering an artificial pathway and timeline. This is not to benefit us but to pervert our natural collective process.

Today we can see that virtual reality headsets can act like a drug, increasing self-absorption and egomaniacal tendencies while creating false neural pathways that are biologically disconnecting us further from soul/spiritual realities. By means of televisions, computers, various frequency weapons and hidden technologies we are constantly being hacked, attuned and calibrated to virtual reality (VR) even when we sleep. Many people have been noticing changes in their dreaming or sleep states.

They are dumbing us down, blurring the lines between the real and the unreal to harness our energy, manipulate our minds and invade our consciousness. People do not understand the deeper implications and applications of the technologies that they are surrounding themselves with. We are essentially energetic beings and with certain subtle body implants we can be reconfigured and harnessed by these beings for consciousness transference.

People are being hacked and seduced into a virtual reality that imitates our true multidimensional potentiality and structures, both personal and planetary. It is a very poor imitation indeed but while most of the populace remains in the dark in regards to true ascension dynamics and in the contrived confusion of the collective moment, these alien intelligences are attempting to assimilate and permanently graft us into a 'false light world' of their creation. These fallen intelligences want us to bypass our true evolutionary potential while tempting us with pseudo-clairvoyant abilities and super powers within their digitised and augmented reality.

We are in fact powerful manifestors, and these fallen intelligences have been manipulating us to misuse our creative abilities (with them) in line with their agenda so we create certain energetic bonds to our detriment, eventually trapping our consciousness through their digital portals. People do not fully comprehend that through certain technologies, under the guise of creating a global Wi-Fi network, we can be easily tracked, targeted and possibly pulsed out from our gross material bodies into digital avatars of ourselves, without perhaps even knowing that we have entered an inorganic false reality or have been steered down an artificially controlled timeline.

As We Awaken

As we awaken, we have the potential to reclaim our latent multidimensional abilities organically and naturally. If people remain distracted, self-absorbed and materially identified, as Earth transitions into its new station of identity they will forfeit the process with her. This planet is ascending, but while most people remain unaware of the possibility and dynamics of true ascension, they are unable to comprehend what is happening.

In the light of what has been shared in these pages, it is hoped that more people will see the need to demand full alien disclosure. The dangers of the misapplication and cost of all this advancing technology, when truly considered, very much outweighs its social positives. In the hands of these elitist rulers who dominate our current social structure or a controlling alien reality, people are only heading towards a multidimensional disaster.

There is a silent war being waged against humanity at this time and this author is the first to admit his naivety in terms of understanding much of what is taking place here on Earth today. Having seen and experienced much more than perhaps what defines the parameters of this small book, these writings are still limited and partial in terms of synthesizing certain experiences and understandings into the greater picture that he and others who are awakening are bearing witness to. Again, it is important for people to understand that it is at times not easy to relate or introduce certain transcendental and multidimensional experiences into our limited constructs of reality. We are dealing with intelligences and realities that exist in a far greater cosmological framework than what much of humanity is used to dealing with.

However, the purpose of this book is to get readers to question the reality that is presented to them, and for this these writings will serve that purpose.

A MADDENING WORLD

We live in a time of bifurcating realities and people are making choices that will affect their future incarnations and stations in this multidimensional universe.

Unfortunately, in the rising tempo of the ongoing planetary catharsis, there is a great lack of awareness as to what is truly happening on Earth at this time. With higher frequencies entering Earth, karmic processes are accelerating and many people are experiencing rising dramas, pressure and pains that come with these planetary shifts as well as other associated ascension symptoms. In this time of change, rifts, misunderstandings and blow-outs between people, groups, families and nations may come to a head or be brought to the surface to be cleared.

There are many people with many different views on what is right for the planet and what is right for humanity at this time and there are many beings with different agendas and investments in the world at present. However, if there is no real understanding of what is truly taking place on Earth in regards to our planetary ascension, there will be a lot of confusion and conflict as to what course of action humanity should take and how we should truly assist Earth and each other.

Taking advantage of this time of collective vulnerability and bewilderment, certain malevolent intelligences, beings and groups on and off-planet seek to utilise, stimulate and exacerbate global confusion and suffering for manipulation purposes, to achieve their own ends. In doing so, these intelligences know that people in fear and self-preservation will do and allow much they would normally think inconceivable. This fear can be easily channelled by those who control society, often against the very people who are truly assisting it.

We live in a very hostile environment at present for those who seek to disclose truthful information on what is happening on the planet right now. Many people who have been attempting to assist the race by revealing what is really going on behind the scenes of our global society and corporate structures, are increasingly being murdered, tortured and imprisoned. We hear of strange or sudden deaths in the truth movement, missing or murdered political and environmental activists and anyone getting close to revealing child trafficking or organ harvesting rings run by the elite that now proliferate around the planet. Many scared people who have come forward telling the public they are being threatened or targeted by certain agencies end up in car accidents, with heart attacks, radiation poisoning, cancer or go insane. If people would look a little deeper and research a little better, they would grow more suspicious with what is going on around them at present and they would see that many of the storylines we are being fed through the media reek with the smell of cover-ups, lies and corruption.

The highly controlled corporate mainstream media says very little and is often used to hide, twist and even completely fabricate the truth of the many strange happenings and global events that are transpiring around us. Most of the public are so completely unaware and so self-absorbed that they are very easily manipulated through the official storylines and sensationalist dialogues given them by the media and those 'higher-ups' in power and authority. In the unveiling nature of our current reality, we must see through the myriad lies and deceptions constantly used to hide what is really happening in the world at present. We should also look within and see the lies we tell ourselves, which are usually to keep a sense of personal control or comfort.

More people are recognising that our entire global society is structured in such a way as to defend and protect the very criminals and miscreants who are ruling and controlling the race and who often mercilessly attack anyone who they deem a threat to their agenda. For this, they have an army of lawyers and unlimited resources to stall, divert or quash any legal proceedings that they might acquire and a police force and military that unquestioningly protect them. This usually comes under the terms of 'upholding the law, keeping the peace or peacekeeping.'

Today in their blindness, many people ridicule almost anything that goes counter to what they have been officially told or manipulated to believe is true. The title 'conspiracy theorist' has become a programmed anathema in society and people who are so labelled are constantly mocked, harassed or associated with psychosis. Reputable scientists and medical professionals, who speak out against the pharmaceutical industry or with their findings counter mainstream medical consensus, are shunned by certain 'official' journals, peers and the public. Government and corporate whistle-blowers find themselves attacked or imprisoned. There are many respectable, genuine and creditable people in science, academia, government and military who are seeking alien/extra-terrestrial disclosure that are ridiculed and mocked. It is strange that one's credibility can be so easily and completely stripped in the minds of the population even though many of those who are revealing such things can rationally and coherently provide true evidence or experience otherwise.

There are also many reasons why the public themselves would try to suppress the revelations and truths emerging from the cracks of our wayward society. Often when people are fractured or in fear, they will bury themselves in the mundane. Hiding from the emerging and unpleasant truths of their current reality they will invest much in our wayward society and its programmed belief systems through which they try to define or distract themselves. Losing their inner connection and unable to discern the deeper reality behind the things and events that move them, they will embrace an indoctrinated society's definition of reality, even if its value and belief system is artificial and anti-life. They will oppose any emerging truths that are counter to their illusions and defend them by whatever means they can, rather than look within and make the needed change.

However, this is a choice. People must understand that everything we do has consequences and all we do against what we know in our deeper heart as right and against universal law, has ramifications. Our reality is multidimensional and behind much of what people see and experience through the mundane senses are forces and intelligences that seek to use and exploit people's selfishness, arrogance and ignorance. If we align with these wayward intelligences through our actions and decisions, then we can make certain energetic bonds and contracts to our detriment. If we refuse to do what we know in our heart as true and right, we become consubstantial with those hidden darker forces and intelligences.

Warren Sunkar

Looking Across the Battlefield

When we look out into the world with only our 3D eyes, we do not see or understand the multidimensional play that is happening around us. Through our fall into deeper density, we have lost much of our sight and perceptions of the subtle and hidden worlds that constantly interplay with our perceived reality. Most of our wounded and materialistically bound humanity have become so confused and fearful that they would refuse to even consider this. However, just because many people refuse to recognise these things does not mean they are not affected by the vast sea of subtle energies and intelligences that permeate and play around us.

Without basic insight into the dynamics and workings of our multidimensional universe and knowledge of the alien takeover bid, we find ourselves as the helpless pawns of those forces, beings and intelligences that we do not recognise. We can become slaves to miscreant agendas crafted by unknown hands. Those of us with the eyes to see know that people are often unknowingly used as instruments or portals for dark and dubious entities. In these strange times, mind control runs most of our society and occult possession has become a normal reality here on earth today.

As new Life energies enter the planet, they are bringing to light many things that have been hidden from human eyes and understanding. The planetary veils are being lifted and many miscreant and misaligned energies are being purged and brought to the surface as part of the planetary rectification. In the rising tempo of today's planetary catharsis, the subtle planes of Earth are being cleared and certain entities in their desperation are gripping, attacking and possessing people in their attempt to hold their placement and position on Earth. People who are ignorant and vulnerable often end up possessed or aligned with miscreant intelligences and find themselves unknowingly being used as conduits or tools for these entities, which are doing everything they must to preserve their way of life by whatever means they can.

Lack of right understanding about the nature of reality and knowledge of the subtle realms and the many types of entities that exist around us is costing humanity dearly. There is a true science to right living which protects us from the unknown and unseen elements of our reality but people over latter generations have mostly rejected hearing these truths when it has collided with their own illusions or self-centred agendas. Again, this is their choice but today the fury and madness of the hellish realms is being increasingly unleashed on those unsuspecting, with the more selfishly inclined being used to further the nefarious agendas of those who wield various energies from their stations of power. Often those possessed are ignorant as to how they are being used, often working counter to the divine evolutionary plan for Earth or against those people who are truly assisting the planet during this time of ascension.

Most people in our modern society have been programmed over generations to believe that black magic and occult sciences are fantasy or illusory and thus believe they do not affect them. This is gross ignorance. While today's public are often fed rationalist, atheistic and materialistic programs and themes in denial of their holistic reality, certain global leaders are well versed in occult dynamics and black magic, using people as their pawns against the planet and each other. Through hidden networks of secret societies and magic circles, they plan and implement their various endeavours and the public are used to ignorantly participate and support their despotic agendas.

Mainstream religion will not truly educate the public at all about these things because it is controlled through its hierarchy by the very same dark forces. People need to recognise that many of those in positions of power are consciously engaged in secretive black magic and occult groups who use their knowledge against the public for various agendas. Over the decades their membership has been steadily growing around the world.

An example of this is Hollywood, which over recent years, has been increasingly exposed as a haven for Satanist groups engaged in human trafficking, paedophilia and satanic ritual abuse. Working covertly with the alien controlled, military industrial complex, it is a major centre for global mind control, with many actors knowingly participating in an occult war against the human race. If people would take a step back and more deeply analyse what is happening, they would realise that almost all entertainment emanating from this mainstream source is usually created to manipulate, dehumanise and denigrate the global population in some way or form.

However, most people are unable to discern what is happening and are unaware of how things work. They do not comprehend that almost every aspect of their current lives has been manipulated and crafted to control and abuse them. The public are too shut down and unable to comprehend the warfare strategies being used against them, or recognise that their mundane lives have been almost completely contrived to make them the loyal and willing agents of these involuntary forces.

Metaphysical and occult sciences in general reveal the deeper workings and structure of our multidimensional universe and reality. They shouldn't be feared but should be deeply respected. However, these sciences of universal laws and dynamics have often been twisted and misused by various intelligences and beings for selfish purposes, sometimes at a horrendous cost to themselves and the planet. These dark intelligences understand the unified field in which we live and know that just one act of evil can affect many other aspects of our reality. In their madness and meanness they often seek to pervert, weaken, hinder and harm as much as they can get away with, to keep people under control and subjugation. They seek every opportunity to exploit our wounds and pain to their advantage.

Those who are regaining their multidimensional sight, see a host of dubious and miscreant cosmic entities and intelligences working as one vast collective of evil, working together to exploit Earth and its humanity. The writer of this work has encountered and sometimes collided with demons, greys, reptilians, fallen angelics, black hole gods and fallen metatronic intelligence. These beings are hostile and with a large variety of tricks, subtle weaponry and technologies at their disposal. It is these diabolic intelligences that are using the world controllers to achieve their goals within these lower densities.

It is important that we gain a deeper perspective of what is out there in terms of our universal structure and understand the mess that it is in. Then we will come to more deeply understand this hierarchy of intelligent evil that is infecting the world at present and we will see the deeper importance on where we put our energies and how we conduct ourselves in the world. If people choose to stay ignorant of these realities they will be easily used and, under cosmic law, held accountable to what they have participated in. Ignorance is not bliss and people must learn how the choices they make each day affect them within our greater cosmic structure and determine their possible future.

How We Disempower Ourselves

Today in this landscape of contrived fear and confusion we are seeing heightened aggression at everything that is not in mainstream acceptance or political correctness. Under increasing pressure and seeming threat from their environment, people's ability to coherently think and deal with problems is greatly diminished. The use of certain hidden technologies and mind control are slowly eroding and destroying people's minds and subtle faculties while channelling them into controlled outcomes so they remain unaware that they are being used and attacked. Under the demoralisation and dehumanisation tactics of current world controllers, the global population itself is being pummelled into submission.

This writer has said that people in self-preservation will often do and allow that which they would normally think inconceivable. Unable to cope with these rising pressures of a maddening world, people will often retreat into self and lash out blindly or attack those who they perceive as threatening to their self-centred bubbles of reality. In such fear they are easily coerced or manipulated to do things that are against their inherent soul nature, and when people do this, they wound their inner being. Not wanting to recognise or deal with the inner pain that has been created by going against what they intrinsically know is right, they seek to continually override their conscience by refusing to acknowledge the harm they are causing others or themselves through their actions and choices. Such people refuse to look within and often need to point the finger or cast blame on others to relieve their growing inner anxiety. It is these wounded or soul fractured people who often become the most aggressive recruits of the takeover agenda as they seek to destroy and muffle anything that reminds them of their inner pain.

People in such self-defence do not want to face the lies they are continually living, and in doing so they often make things much worse for themselves. Eventually, through the continual overriding of their conscience and what they know is true and right, they find themselves becoming consubstantial with the hierarchy of intelligent evil that is today exerting itself to the upmost. It is these people who are being wielded as easily possessed agents for a growing army of darkness that is taking over the planet.

Misery loves company and the walking wounded often group together and support each other to perpetuate their illusions. They refuse to recognise or acknowledge the truth of their collective situation because it means admitting one's own participation in supporting the growing madness and evil of these times. This is the fear our present global society is in denial of, and over many lifetimes of progressively refusing to acknowledge the truth of their wayward realities, people have helped create a global Babylon.

Those people who have profited from or invested much in our modern society will ignore deeper truths and often turn their backs on the evil happening around them, mostly to save themselves from their own exposure. However, under the pressure that the new life energies are bringing, their lives are becoming more difficult, chaotic and suffocating. In the rising tempo of planetary change these people will possibly self-destruct, and unless they go within and resolve their issues and heal their inner pain they will completely remove themselves from the current opportunity of true ascension.

These are the things that the world ego is struggling with at this time and people are making their choices.

As our society has been put under increasing pressure, attacks on genuine and truth seeking people have become more open and aggressive. People should ask themselves, What am I hiding?

No one should have to fear or put up with any form of intimidation from anyone when they are sincere, coherent and well-experienced in what they are describing, exchanging or presenting. Sincere, intelligent and open dialogue is a way to expand our consciousness and grow as a race. People who harass, attack and belittle those who are genuinely seeking to be of service to the race, should look within at their true motives and they will see what is truly controlling them.

Divine servers are no strangers to intimidation here on planet Earth. Unfortunately, many of us have had to put up with threats and abuse from the public who lack deeper discernment and honesty, or have been streamlined or brainwashed to often fear and attack that which lies beyond their limited and often programmed perceptions of reality. People do not understand that in trying to save themselves from exposure, they become truly disempowered and eventually consubstantial with those darker intelligences that use people's selfishness to serve their own ends.

Intimidation and Attacks

It is important for people to get a deeper comprehension of the tactics and attacks that are being used against people who are seeking to maintain their soul/spiritual alignments and service in a world that is mostly anti-life. Attacks can come in many different forms and guises and for a variety of reasons, though underlying them all is self-preservation by the aggressor. They can be varied and multiform, from overt and hidden quarters, against individuals or groups and are usually initiated from the subtle spheres. They can come as public slander or harassment by people, through mainstream or online media. They can be in the form of legal threats, lengthy and costly law suits. They can come through various aggressors, from close or distant relations, and range in spectrum from mockery, harassment and intimidation to physical attack and murder.

Other attacks can come in the form of magical and psychic attacks. This is commonly used as a method by those elite and black magicians in compacts with demonic entities, and is being increasingly directed against people of interest, star-seeds and divine servers. People are often used and possessed by certain entities to carry out various strikes. If people would understand that sometimes the tragic events they read in their newspapers often have hidden origins and causes, they would not be so quick or harsh in their judgements and opinions of events.

Not so well-known at present but coming to the foreground of the collective consciousness, is the increasing use of psychotronic weapons for harassment and targeting. There is a multitude of frequency weaponry, subtle technology and devices wielded by both alien and covert human military groups, on both gross and subtle planes. People need to understand that the deeper hidden structures of the military industrial complex are secretly working together with alien intelligence through either compartmentalised association or direct contact.

Frequency weaponry is often called slow or soft-kill weaponry and is part of a strategy of silent warfare used against the human populace to avoid detection. Many people do not understand that their computers, cell phones and smart devices are weaponised and used for many different reasons. Cell phone towers can direct a variety of harmful or deadly frequencies to target individuals and whole populations. Many people today are complaining about such targeting and harassment but are ignored by the media and the disbelieving public in general.

This author over many years has worked with many highly acclaimed and respected writers, speakers and professionals around the world and has personally known, spoken to and worked with several such people who said they were being targeted in various ways. These were good, intelligent and healthy people, doing work exposing corruption or in divine service that died of sudden illness, lost their sanity or committed suicide. If people would look at the information these people were presenting or exposing, they would perhaps observe that there was much more going on other than the explanations that were officially known or given. Here is a real hint. Look beyond the words conspiracy theory, cult and looney and you might just discover a few things. There are real tragedies and murders occurring in full public view, yet hidden in plain sight.

People must understand that those who are truly waking up, going counter to mainstream consensus reality, and in particular those few true spiritual leaders scattered across the planet, are often being attacked in various ways and by various means. I have spoken to many well-educated and coherent presenters, academics and leaders who have survived or encountered such attacks and this writer himself has over the years survived several attempts on his life and multiple attempts of character assassination.

Those who wish to be of true service to the race should understand its current disposition and social climate. The enemy often seeks to isolate individual servers and groups to keep them constantly harassed, intimidated or ineffective. It is easy to stir public opinion against anyone bringing forth truthful revelations and information by using confusion, lies, intimidation and all sorts of propaganda. People should understand that often through their own misdirected and misinformed opinions, much poison is spread and this is how the public is often used to participate in the attack, cover-up and confusion surrounding the targeting and killing of certain individuals.

True servers are not swayed by public opinion and ridicule but people in their ignorance and blindness often add to the many hardships and drama of assisting a planet in need. Thus people disempower themselves by attacking and threatening those who have come in true divine assistance. Not understanding or caring about what they do, their energies rebound and in the end many people have made circumstances much harder for themselves.

What We Align With

People need to understand that we live in a world that is directed by unseen forces and intelligences, and it is about these realities that people must learn to live better to protect themselves.

One of the greatest weapons that the forces of darkness use is our very selves. It is we who are mobilised against the Earth and each other in our fear, ignorance and selfishness. When we act against what we inherently know as true and right we damage ourselves and each other, which leaves us vulnerable and open to greater manipulation and eventually possession by these wayward intelligences and realities.

People need to face their fears and be honest with themselves to bring about the greater healing they need to change their wayward lives. Then, they need not be scared or intimidated by the seeming madness rising in the world around them but see the importance of coming into greater alignment with universal laws and seek the true nature of reality. Eventually, people will learn how to truly support each other.

But it is important to look within and see what truly motivates us.

We are all participants in this great play at present, and it would be wise to understand the forces and energies that you are resonating with. Every day, every moment the choices and decisions we make are affecting our future destinies. If we are willing to face what needs to be faced within ourselves and make a sincere and selfless effort to live in alignment with the true divine plan, then we will eventually find ourselves naturally consubstantial with those selfless and beneficent divine forces and intelligences who will give us the necessary assistance and protection.

This is how we become truly empowered.

THE NEW HORIZON

Whether humanity chooses to believe it or not we exist in a conscious, multidimensional universal structure that exists within a greater multi-universal reality. This implies that there are laws that govern and run our universe so that it keeps its integrity and stability to host the innumerable beings, worlds and realities that exist and evolve within it. It is also important that beings and species learn to harmonise with these laws to live healthy, balanced and evolutionary lives in alignment with their own inherent purpose within our vast cosmic structure. This is how we evolve and return home to the divine universe.

However, certain beings through various cosmic events and choices have sought to distort and corrupt this universal patterning to suit their own miscreant agendas. This has dramatically affected the safety, stability and free will of many species on Earth and throughout the universe. This wayward course of decisions and actions can only be permitted for so long in-line with certain universal laws as necessary lessons are learnt by various beings that they may change their ways and re-join the divine evolutionary stream. Eventually, however, all must be brought into account and rectification.

Our Earth is watched and attended to by divine agencies and beings who have over time sought to bring it back into harmony and alignment with its true divine purpose. The excessive tampering and manipulation of Earth and its populations by malevolent off-world forces has brought about a necessary response from divine and benevolent intelligences from our universe and beyond. If our planet's wayward course had been allowed to continue, it would have been disastrous not just for Earth and its humanity but for many other worlds and realities in our solar system and beyond.

Modern humanity does not understand that extra-terrestrials have often visited Earth and continue to do so. In fact people will soon face the possibility that their true origins are extra-terrestrial. However, the human race has forgotten this and been unknowingly held for a long time in a consciousness prison by beings of a malevolent nature, who have been secretly stealing planetary resources and exploiting them as a food source.

Today in response, we are bearing witness to the advent and influx of many divine servers coming from various parts of our universal system and beyond to assist in our planetary re-awakening. This is one aspect of the divine intervention at this point in time, and over the next 900 years Earth will be experiencing corrective adjustments and energies in alignment with our galaxy's ongoing healing and realignments.

Although today we are given extraordinary cosmic assistance, this does not absolve humanity of its own responsibilities, and each being is answerable for their actions and alignments. It will be up to people to make the necessary changes within and without, to keep in synchronisation and harmony with these progressive planetary changes. If people themselves choose wilful ignorance in denial of their spiritual realities and what they inwardly know is right, then there is little that can be done for them. It is possible that many people might live out their lives in blindness or total misunderstanding to the events that are transpiring around them. Those who do not make the necessary adjustments and changes in their lives and work in alignment with the planetary ascension processes will find themselves unable to incarnate back onto this ascending planet in the future.

The Divine Correction

Our physical planetary structure is built upon successive manifestation templates that are interlaced and layered with living energetic fields that are interwoven with our greater multidimensional cosmic structure through a subtle planetary grid system. It is this grid system that interpenetrates our Earth and extends out and connects into the greater cosmic structure and holds, reflects, maintains and regulates the incoming cosmic light, energies and information through which we experience our given reality.

As a result of the severe tampering and intentional destruction of our planets grid system by certain alien factions, our planet and its grid system had become very badly damaged. Many of its star-gates and portals had become inactive, destroyed or controlled by various alien factions, and many of its energetic grid lines distorted, broken and redirected. As humans share a sympathetic multidimensional anatomy with their planet, this wilful perversion and destruction of our planetary matrix was used to shut down humanity's connections to the greater cosmos and limit its reality.

People should understand that what they have experienced as 'life' here on earth has been but a small and distorted perception and spectrum of their greater multidimensional reality. Due to certain events, alien tampering and their off-planet AI machinery, our earth became very misaligned with our greater universal reality. Such misalignment had caused all sorts of complications, one being that the cosmic light which refracts against Earth's magnetic grid had been distorted, and this greatly obscured and limited people's ability to coherently perceive and experience their greater multidimensional reality. This affected people's ability to interact with 'reality' by its true design. The result has been that people have been trapped in one big illusion for a very long time, cut off from their greater cosmic reality, having been forced into continuous reincarnation cycles to play out repetitive programmes over and over through successive lives of self-destructive karmic patterning.

In short, humanity has been continuously recycled within these lower densities, unable to progress on its true evolutionary journey.

This is now changing.

Over the last decade certain ascension fail-safes were triggered within the planetary structure which will progressively allow for the healing and transmutation of the planet in line with the ongoing and greater galactic healing that is taking place at this time. Over the course of the next 900 years, Earth will experience various energies and adjustments to produce successive healings and changes. Humanity will necessarily be going through deep catharsis, changes and expansion of consciousness in alignment with the planet and with an assortment of effects and ramifications.

Today as these changes progress, more and more people are reclaiming certain lost or latent multidimensional faculties and various clairvoyant abilities. Certain people are remembering their divine missions that were inaugurated pre-natal from higher spheres for being on earth at this time. Increasing numbers of people are contacting and travelling to other realities, worlds, times and dimensions. As planetary veils lift, much is being revealed in terms of our perceived planetary reality, and it will be up to people to make their choices and alignments as to how they wish to experience these times of great change and ascension.

At this point it is also pertinent to mention that the divine plan is a living plan and has been subject to many adjustments. It is an incorporate plan that includes many worlds, beings and realities. On Earth it works in with humanity's collective and individual choices, as well as responding to other-worldly interferences and choices made by off-world beings and realities. Its vast scope and measure extends far beyond the correction of our linear time-space realties that have been lived down here on Earth. As required, there have been many changes made in recent times.

The original plan for Earth and its humanity was one of reclamation of those lost and fallen beings back to Tara (the 5D station of Earth identity). However, due to interference from cosmic evil at even higher levels of being and identity, the plan has been adapted and changed in several ways. The intelligence and design of cosmic evil, knowing the plan of this reclamation attempt, was to allow servers to incarnate into lower stations of identity with the intention to ensnare them

– if not here on current Earth then in future stations of identity.

However, there have been plans within plans, and foreseeing this as a possible circumstance, certain divine agencies set forth to counter these possibilities. With the agreement of Mother Earth, the activation of certain planetary fail-safes were implemented through stealth over the last decade and Earth will be ascending back into the inner planes of creation over the ensuing period. This is ascension into the *deific* planes of inner creation, and for those who are working on this ascending timeline, it will involve a change in rotation of particle spin to continue with the planet and its processes. Here on earth this has meant that things will proceed a little differently and faster than perhaps what some servers and star-seeds have understood or anticipated.

Many star-seeds and people are still caught in the impulses and play of the original plan. However, we are called to adapt to the changing mission at this time. Those who are unable to change and are caught in the inertia of their original missions, will still find themselves ascending to higher stations of identity but within realities that could possibly still be in a fall state. The original 5D ascension plan was aborted by its true planetary guardians due to heavy alien manipulation and is now a false ascension timeline. However, we have been given a short period of grace as a greater window of opportunity is being extended to those who are receptive at this time to make the needed changes.

Mother Earth is a conscious being with her own evolutionary pathway and she has chosen her path. It is important that people get a deeper context of reality and understanding as to how and why they incarnated here on Earth at this time, as many beings have incarnated from our greater cosmic structure that have come to Earth to assist. If we choose to ascend with her, we must make the necessary adjustments to our current lives. It will be up to us to stay in synch with oncoming Earth changes and energies, working co-creatively and consciously with true divine intelligence.

At present, there is a parting of ways, and those people who are unable or refuse to change their misaligned and selfish dispositions will soon find themselves unable to reincarnate on this ascension planet. These beings must be transferred elsewhere in the cosmos in alignment with their choices and decisions because they will find it increasingly difficult to live in the higher vibrational terrain that Earth is becoming.

In their desperation to maintain their control, certain alien species and human elite have been poisoning and hurting the Earth and steadily imposing a global technocratic prison system with designs to trick and trap humanity into a shadow world of their own design. These beings and intelligences have continued to counter every progressive and beneficent change on the planet and things have become greatly complicated and confused here on Earth at this time. People must learn to see beyond the movie version of events and the false narratives that are given them through various media to distract and confuse them. Our reality is multidimensional and what we experience on earth usually originates from unseen causes that are beyond our mundane perceptions and experiences of reality. We are often unknowingly used to play out the various dramas of a warring cosmic reality being furiously fought around us.

Things are not what they seem. As people awaken they will realise that many of the wars, atrocities and depravities being fought or committed today under various guises, are in fact struggles of alien dominance over certain portals and strategic places or territories of the earth with most of the human military unsuspecting on how they are being used or manipulated.

People must comprehend that almost any official explanation given in these times to many world events and dramas are simply cover stories for greater dimensional happenings and conflicts that are taking place in these times. Often it is these explanations that form the general beliefs and consensus reality of a highly manipulated and mind controlled public who are being totally misled. Reading the morning newspaper or watching the TV, people passionately debate, argue and quarrel over their various opinions and perceptions, believing themselves informed. However, without a greater multidimensional perspective their understandings are very partial and their views errant. All this simply reinforces various false narratives and perspectives that provide the very cover for alien intelligences.

As events unfold around us in the coming years we will need a much deeper context for what is happening on the planet. It is important to see how our very belief structures have been highly manipulated and how they have stopped us from actualising our greater potentiality. If we do not come to more deeply comprehend the multidimensional universal structure in which we live, our own multidimensional anatomy and the truth of the alien takeover, then we will not understand what is happening. We will continue to be confused and ineffective to produce the changes we need within ourselves to stay in line with planetary ascension processes. We should not be afraid to carefully explore the new even if this means re-assessing all what we once believed, especially in the deeper understanding that what we have known, or what we thought we knew, has only ever been distorted or very partial.

Taking Self-Responsibility

In the light of what has been presented in this book, people are offered a different perspective on what is happening in the world today. As portions of our global population awaken and reclaim their multi-dimensional faculties, they will see the need to take greater responsibility for their lives and how each day and moment they are making choices and taking actions that shall determine their future paths. If we stay in ignorance of our greater potentialities, or allow others to dictate or control our reality, we become disempowered and are dragged into circumstances and timelines that might inevitably lead to being removed from our true evolutionary processes completely.

People need to change their ways and those who are on ascending timelines understand the importance of putting God first in their lives. This reverses our habitual selfish tendencies to have us focus up and beyond the personality nature in service and alignment with the true Divine Plan. When we honour the divine in all things and truly put others before ourselves, our true ascension processes start. This is how our metaphysical horizon broadens and how we naturally unfold our inherent multidimensional capabilities. If we stay self-orientated and self-focused, all higher knowledge of ascension and universal dynamics is basically useless and will only harm us and the planet because one's intent is wayward and its applications will become distorted and confused.

We become truly empowered the more we seek and strive to live in greater accordance with our true divine nature. As we awaken the eye of the soul, we leave the consciousness constraints and limitations of our personality nature and see through those illusions and programmed belief structures that dominate current society. We can then more consciously choose where we put our time and energy with better understanding as to how we are to live on our ascending planet. Over time we will earn a deeper sense of freedom. When this is done in right divine alignment, we naturally magnetise all what we truly need in the moment and attract those true benevolent forces and intelligences that seek to protect, help and guide us through these times. We can move beyond the manipulation and control of those selfish alien realities.

In the growing awareness of our multidimensional universal structure and our place within the greater cosmic reality, we need to live harmoniously and healthily with the many diverse life forms we share our universe with. Humanity needs to let go of those personal and collective arrogances and adopt a deeper sense of humility and attentiveness to the changing landscape around them. This does not mean subservience but a healthy respect and awareness for all sentient beings and intelligences in their uniqueness and diversity. We must healthily incorporate our growing spectrums of awareness while honouring our own inner integrity and staying in right divine alignment. We can regain our cosmic citizenship as true planetary custodians and this is how we will gain increasing access to our greater cosmic multidimensional structure.

The author of this book is aware that much of what is written in these pages will be hard to digest for many who are still defined by the lineal and closed parameters of their current materially based society. However, in a little time, Life itself will reveal the truth of certain things. Whether people care to make the necessary shifts and adjustments within themselves or not, our world is fast changing. If people ignore the many signs around them, then the coming period will be possibly one of confusion and fear. Change is constant and inevitable, and whatever form the worldly drama takes, it is important to remember that we are all going through this together in one great catharsis and healing.

What is more is that for those who are open and vigilant, there is also amazing opportunity. We have the unique capability over the ensuing years, to host ourselves home. In synchronisation and alignment with the incoming energies and ongoing planetary changes, we now have the possibility to go way beyond that which was originally intended for humanity at this planetary juncture.

There is much more that could be written in these pages. However, the intent of these writings has been to highlight the need for a serious re-evaluation of our planetary circumstances and to assist people into a perspective shift that will benefit their greater journey.

A Little *More* Light From The Stars

We are collectively going through a radical time of change and it is desirable that people see the need to work together.

It is intended that these writings will inspire people to look beyond the mundane, to seek the deeper truths of our existence and to ask themselves the important questions. We are all in a time of amazing and incredible discovery, and it is hoped that people will not be afraid to question the very foundations of what they have thought as reality and that this little book may be that starting point.

God Bless!

www.ingramcontent.com/pod-product-compliance
Lightning Source LLC
Chambersburg PA
CBHW070737020526
44118CB00035B/1411